CONTENTS

NOT STRANGERS
BUT PILGRIMS

The Next Steps for

CHURCHES TOGETHER
IN PILGRIMAGE

Including definitive proposals for
ecumenical instruments

Published jointly by the British Council of Churches and
the Catholic Truth Society for the Inter-Church Process
Not Strangers but Pilgrims

ISBN 0 85169 139 0 (BCC)
ISBN 0 85183 774 3 (CTS)

Published for the Inter-Church Process
Not Strangers but Pilgrims
by the British Council of Churches
Inter-Church House,
35-41 Lower Marsh,
London, SE1 7RL
and the Catholic Truth Society
38-40 Eccleston Square,
London, SW1V 1PD.

Designed by Gooderham Bate
Printed by Design & Print, Shoreham-by-Sea, West Sussex

1 LETTER OF COMMENDATION TO THE CHURCHES

The Not Strangers but Pilgrims Inter-Church Process began in 1985, and since then our partnership in pilgrimage has been much blessed, whether in large gatherings such as Nottingham, Bangor, St. Andrews and Swanwick, or in the many smaller ecumenical groups associated with Lent '86 and similar projects.

Faith, not sight, is what characterises pilgrimage, but the blessings we have so far enjoyed give us confidence in our journey into the future. Anglican, Baptist, Black-led Pentecostal and Holiness Churches, Congregational, Lutheran, Methodist, Orthodox, Roman Catholic and Reformed Churches have been taking part in this Inter-Church Process (for the full list see p.105). On behalf of their representatives on the Inter-Church Meeting, which I chair, I commend to all the participating churches, their formal meetings and their individual members, the proposals in this booklet for our "Next Steps Together in Pilgrimage". Please study it and respond to it hopefully and prayerfully, as we ask God to guide us on the next stage of our pilgrimage.

John Habgood
Chairman
Inter-Church Meeting

2 INTRODUCTION

*O Lord God, when thou givest to thy servants to
endeavour any great matter, grant us to know that it is
not the beginning but the continuing of the same, until it
be thoroughly finished, which yieldeth
true glory.*

The Inter-Church Process *Not Strangers but Pilgrims* is founded on the willingness of the participating churches to enter into a commitment to one another, already expressed by their representatives in the Swanwick declaration, extending far beyond anything that has gone before. This requires a shift in the thinking, feeling and action of our churches "from ecumenism as an extra, which absorbs energy, to ecumenism as a dimension of all that we do, which releases energy through the sharing of resources." This shift needs to be effective at all levels and in all places in order to establish a radically new style of working which builds on the creative ecumenical relationships of the many rather than the ecumenical activities of the few.

It is vital that this shift takes place locally, in towns, villages and city areas; and also at what we call the 'intermediate level', where churches work together at Diocesan /presbytery/district/county/borough level. How precisely this shift is to take place needs to be worked out and decided locally; and of course in many places it has already taken place, particularly through the development of local ecumenical projects, local and regional covenants, and area ecumenical councils and assemblies, as well as through ecumenical house groups which especially through Lent '86 and similar events experienced the gift of unity and called for it to be a greater priority for all.

At the local and intermediate levels the development and growth of ecumenically shared life based on this challenging principle brings with it also the need for local churches together in pilgrimage to be resourced and encouraged by denominations *together* rather than separately.

At the national level the churches' public witness together needs to grow out of relationships formed through shared prayer, consultation and resource-sharing.

There will also need to be a conscious act of self-denial by the churches, so that when new work is proposed, in every department of church life at every level, local, intermediate or national, each does not simply go ahead as before, as if no-one else existed. Instead, after due consultation, the churches will need

3

to decide together whether to accept a new proposal, and if so how it should be implemented, whether by sharing the resources of all, or using those of one or more on behalf of the rest. In this way such work will be *owned* by all from the start, and will be reported to the synods and assemblies of all with appropriate recommendations.

The next steps to be taken by churches together in pilgrimage are to do with this new style of working, which the proposed new ecumenical instruments at all levels exist to promote and serve. Nor should it be forgotten that national and intermediate bodies exist to serve local ecumenical life. For the overall purpose of this "inter-church process of prayer, reflection and debate together on the nature and purpose of the church in the light of its mission" is to encourage participation by Christians and churches together in local witness, ministry and mission.

The realisation of these goals lies in the future, and they are not easily attained; what is asked of us now is a shared commitment to strive towards them.

The ecumenical movement is not about some contrived, technical or theological alignment of doctrine and practice between churches, carried out by some group of remote ecclesiastical managers; it must have an experiential, personal, even emotional side to it. That is why local ecumenism is so important. It is in the local church that our denominational strengths lie, and it is in our local churches that our ecumenical relationship are experienced, for ecumenism is about relationships; not relationships we achieve, but relationships we are given; we are "one in Christ" and that must be experienced, and expressed, and have consequences, as our common Basis, printed elsewhere in this booklet, makes plain.

It was this awareness that lay behind the Swanwick Declaration, and that is spelled out in the document "The Context and Content of our Pilgrimage". Unless this awareness is a lively and powerful dynamic in our several churches, the Reports in this booklet may well appear uninteresting and irrelevant. It is to remind us all of this "music" of ecumenism, as well as of its hard and sometimes seemingly intractable "facts" that both the Declaration and the "Context and Content" appear immediately before the Reports.

There then follow sections on Membership, Participation and Representation, Assemblies and National Meetings, Major Gatherings, and Finance, which are common to all the new instruments. These have been written in response to the many requests for as much harmonisation as possible in the revised Reports. This has been continued within the several Reports (e.g. a common Basis) but only as far as proved acceptable to all.

In the 1988 booklet, each of the Reports of the Working Parties carried the authority only of its compilers. In this booklet, as the "letter of commendation" states, the Reports of the Working Parties carry the authority of the Inter-

Church Meeting, for we have endeavoured to integrate the proposals in the national reports with the proposals for the British and Irish instrument.

We undertook, in presenting the "indicative" Reports of 1988, to produce "definitive" Reports in 1989, so that each church would have a sufficiently clear understanding of what it was being asked to respond to. But "definitive" cannot mean "detailed" in any comprehensive sense. We have aimed at "optimum" detail. Too little, would be asking the churches to make inadequately informed, and perhaps irresponsible decisions; too much would be impossible and undesirable. For excessive detail would have produced very long, complex reports, and in church reports, the more you write the less is read! We also recognise that we are in pilgrimage together; in a real sense "we know not where we are going" still less how we are to get there; we must have time and space, in our relationships, for growth in understanding, for learning from experience, for sensitive response to the leading of the Spirit. We accept that, after perhaps five years' experience, a major review will probably be desirable – *"semper reformanda"* applies to ecumenical instruments as well as to churches.

These Reports, then, are being submitted to the decision making bodies of our several churches, each of which has its own characteristic procedures and language. These we respect. Yet is is clearly desirable that each church be asked to respond to the same questions. We have therefore drawn up the following Resolution, leaving each church to re-phrase our language in its own idiom; though the expression may vary, the sense will be the same for all.

RESOLUTION

The †.. agrees to participate in the proposed ecumenical bodies for * .... as a ‡.................
...., as described in the report of the Inter-Church Meeting of 1989 *Churches Together in Pilgrimage*, and in consequence:

agrees that the Inter-Church Meeting, ⁑ and in Scotland and Wales the appropriate equivalent bodies also, may make adjustments in detail to the proposals if the responses from churches make this desirable;

authorises the Inter-Church Meeting, ⁑ and in Scotland and Wales the appropriate equivalent bodies also, if in their view sufficient acceptance of the proposals is received, to appoint Commissioning Committees to bring the new ecumenical bodies into existence, including the appointment of senior officers;

authorises the Inter-Church Meeting, ⁑ and in Scotland and Wales the appropriate equivalent bodies also, on behalf of the participating churches to seek any necessary funding to provide overlap with existing councils; and

requests the existing councils to make such amendments to their constitutions as will facilitate the transition to the new bodies.

† Insert the name of the church or association of churches.

* Insert England, Scotland, Wales, Britain and Ireland as appropriate to the geographical situation of the church concerned, indicating one or more of the nations as well as Britain and Ireland.

‡ Insert the category of membership desired, as set out in Section 5 below on Membership and the relevant sections of the Reports for England, Scotland, Wales, and Britain and Ireland.

⁑ include the relevant part(s) of this clause according to the geographical situation of the church concerned.

By September, 1989 we shall know the responses of almost all the churches. We hope very much that the answer will be "Yes", or at least "Yes – but". If the latter, we shall try to respond and to adjust appropriately. We very much hope that the answer will not be "No – unless", or just plain "No". If the latter, we shall have a major task of "damage limitation", for we shall not be "back at square one", but, disillusioned and disappointed, back at "square one – minus-minus". Please God, it shall not be so; that the answer, in faith and obedience, will be "Yes". Then the Inter-Church Meetings, made up of the appointed representatives of each church, will set up Commissioning Committees with authority from the churches to bring the new ecumenical instruments into being. All this is set out in the Resolution. We hope that, where appropriate, new senior staff will be in post early in 1990 so that existing staff will be able to work with new staff to ensure continuity and carry over of knowledge, memory and relationships as the new instruments come into responsible existence in September 1990.

All this, of course, is very demanding on those serving on the various Commissioning bodies, requiring careful and detailed planning. It is also, for all the churches involved, a high-risk endeavour – which brings us back again to our opening prayer.

Alastair Haggart
Chairman
Steering Group of the Inter-Church Process

3 SWANWICK DECLARATION

The following 'Swanwick Declaration' was adopted by acclaim and personally signed by those present at The Hayes Conference Centre, Swanwick, on Friday 4 September 1987. The Conference asked that it should be read in churches in England, Scotland and Wales on one of the Sundays in October.

No Longer Strangers – Pilgrims!
Nid Dieithriaid Mwyach – Pererinion!
Luchd-Turuis – Conhla!

Appointed by our churches and under the guidance of the Holy Spirit we declare that this, the broadest assembly of British and Irish churches ever to meet in these islands has reached a common mind. We are aware that not all Christians are represented amongst us but we look forward to the time when they will share fully with us.

We came with different experiences and traditions, some with long ecumenical service, some for whom this is a new adventure. We are one band of pilgrims. We are old and young, women and men, black and white, lay and ordained and we travelled from the four corners of these islands to meet at Swanwick in Derbyshire. There we met, we listened, we talked, we worshipped, we prayed, we sat in silence, deeper than words. Against the background of so much suffering and sinfulness in our society we were reminded of our call to witness that God was in Christ reconciling the world to himself. We affirmed that this world with all its sin and splendour belongs to God. Young people called on us to be ready to sort out our priorities so that we could travel light and concentrate on our goal. Driven on by a gospel imperative to seek unity that the world may believe, we rejoiced that we are pilgrims together and strangers no longer.

We now declare together our readiness to commit ourselves to each other under God. Our earnest desire is to become more fully, in his own time, the one Church of Christ, united in faith, communion, pastoral care and mission. Such unity is the gift of God. With gratitude we have truly experienced this gift, growing amongst us in these days. We affirm our openness to this growing unity in obedience to the Word of God, so that we may fully share, hold in common and offer to the world those gifts which we have received and still hold in separation. In the unity we seek we recognise that there will not be uniformity but legitimate diversity.

It is our conviction that, as a matter of policy at all levels and in all places, our churches must now move from co-operation to clear commitment to each other, in search of the unity for which Christ prayed and in common evangelism and service of the world.

We urge church leaders and representatives to take all necessary steps to present, as soon as possible, to our church authorities, assemblies and congregations, the Report of this Conference together with developed proposals for ecumenical instruments to help the churches of these islands to move ahead together.

Continuing to trust in the promised gift of the Holy Spirit, we look forward with confidence to sharing with our own churches the joys of this historic Conference. We thank God for all those who, from Lent '86 and before, have been part of this pilgrimage. We feel their presence with us. We urge our churches to confirm by decision and action the hopes and vision on which we have laid hold, and which we shall not let go.

This is a new beginning. We set out on our further pilgrimage ready to take risks and determined not to be put off by 'dismal stories'. We resolve that no discouragement will make us once relent our avowed intent to be pilgrims together. Leaving behind painful memories and reaching out for what lies ahead, we press on towards the full reconciliation in Christ of all things in heaven and on earth, that God has promised in his Kingdom.

Lord God, we thank you
For calling us into the company
Of those who trust in Christ
And seek to obey his will.
May your Spirit guide and strengthen us
In mission and service to your world;
For we are strangers no longer
But pilgrims together on the way to your Kingdom.
Amen.

4 SWANWICK REPORT: THE CONTEXT AND CONTENT OF OUR PILGRIMAGE

God's World, God's Kingdom

The ecumenical movement begins from the unity of God, and its end is the reconciliation of the world in God.

We believe in one God, Father, Son and Holy Spirit, three Persons in the perfect unity of love. Jesus prayed that his followers might be one as he is one with the Father, so that the world might believe. The Church is called ever more faithfully to realise, embody and express this divinely given unity in a communion of persons united in the love of God.

We believe that God was in Christ reconciling the world to himself, and that he has entrusted this ministry of reconciliation to the church. Christians are sent by God as Christ's ambassadors to continue the mission by which the Father sent the Son to redeem the world and to gather into one the scattered children of God.

The disobedience of humanity to God has consequences that are both personal and social. Sin alienates from God. It also divides society. At a time when scientific and technological progress makes it possible for people and nations to share one another's gifts and to meet one another's needs, we are painfully aware of the divisions between rich and poor, black and white, the powerful and the powerless, and between differing political and ideological systems.

The Church is called to preach the Gospel amid the divisions and opportunities of our world. It has to do this by engaging in evangelism, by serving the poor and dispossessed, by addressing the needs of those exercising power and responsibility in such fields as industry, science and politics, and by standing up for justice and peace before the principalities and powers of this world.

We confess anew with shame, however, that Christians too are divided in various ways. A Church called to God's work of reconciliation in the world will only be credible if it is a body that demonstrates within its own life the reconciling power of Jesus Christ. We cannot do this effectively unless we begin to overcome within the Church not only ecclesiastical and doctrinal, but also social, racial and economic divisions, as well as disunity between the churches.

We live by hope, acknowledging that human sin and division will never be completely overcome in this world even within the Church. The ultimate goal for which Christians pray is the Kingdom of God. Jesus used this phrase to express the mysterious and partly hidden activity of God in the world then and now. It is within us and yet we pray for its accomplishment by God at the end of time. It is one of the mysteries of our faith and Jesus offers us glimpses of what it will be like – the hungry are fed, the homeless are housed, debts are forgiven.

The Church is called by Christ both to embody and to point towards God's Kingdom. To do this effectively, generosity, forgiveness and sacrifice have to be shown within the Church as well as by the Church to the world. This is not easy or cheap. The Way of the Cross is a road that leads to new life. Part of this renewal is the pilgrimage of divided Christians towards closer Christian unity.

The journey already begun

Lent '86 and the Inter-Church Process* have been recognised as important and exciting not only by those of us who attended the Swanwick Conference but also by people at every level in the churches which have participated in them. The Inter-Church Process throughout has been building from the ground upwards, not imposing something from the top downwards. It began largely in response to local ecumenical developments; an essential part of the next stage of the journey was the Lent '86 course for local churches and local radio which also produced *Views from the Pews* for all to hear. In some areas Lent '87 and further local ecumenical developments have continued this movement. The Inter-Church Process moves on after Swanwick into its next phase, of which growing further together locally is an essential part. There is a heartfelt desire for this local dimension to be affirmed and continued; and for resources to be identified in order that lay Christians may be equipped to share their faith in the secular world with those of other faiths and those of none.

The Not Strangers but Pilgrims process has also been built on much painful and painstaking work faithfully done during recent generations starting with Edinburgh 1910 and carried forward via such landmarks as Vatican II and the publication of the Lima report on 'Baptism, Eucharist and Ministry'. The faithful observance of the Week of Prayer for Christian Unity, the work of local, national and international Councils of Churches, the development of covenanted relationships, together with many other steps large and small have brought us to a new realisation that we, Christians from different traditions, are on converging paths. Convergence comes as people meet to affirm their oneness in Christ, to share their faith, to worship and pray together, and so begin to enter into one another's spiritual traditions. Such mutual openness and trust gives us the confidence to turn to one another in penitence for pain inflicted by us and by our forbears, and to turn to the world in common witness to Christ.

The degree of unity already achieved is heartening. The full participation in this Process of the Black-led churches, the Roman Catholic Church and others alongside the existing members of the British Council of Churches gives a new impetus and a fresh enthusiasm to our ecumenical pilgrimage. Although more distant goals of fuller unity are not yet clear, we affirm our readiness to progress beyond co-operation to mutual commitment in the search for closer and closer unity in Christ.

Spirituality and Authority

The Inter-Church Process has deepened our understanding of one another and of Christ's call to proclaim the Gospel. In our worship and reflection together we have come to realise the deep bonds of faith that unite us in Christ. At the same time we have come to see the differences between us more clearly. We have a deeper appreciation of the visible and historical characteristics of each church and denomination. There are differences of doctrine and discipline, of spirituality and patterns of worship. We need to acknowledge both the things that unite us and those that divide us if the Inter-Church Process is to take us on the path to unity in truth and love. As we travel the way of Pilgrims we must continue to study together the important issues that divide us (e.g. the nature of the church, authority, ministry) and celebrate the gift of that unity which we have already received.

God declares his will through his Word. We are called to believe in him, follow him and obey him. We grow in faith, hope and love when we come together to hear and celebrate God's Word. We need to explore new, creative and shared forms of worship. Worshipping together and sharing one another's worship deepens the spiritual bonds between us and nourishes our common witness. While this is a positive experience for many, we all recognise that our different

*See further,
Views from the Pews: Lent '86 and Local Ecumenism: BCC/CTS
Reflections: How churches see their life and mission: BCC/CTS
Observations on the Church from Britain and abroad: BCC/CTS

understandings of the Eucharist create barriers which for many are very serious and painful. We need to explore urgently the ways in which we can express in our worship that unity in Christ which we already have. Together we need to seek to understand the place of the Eucharist in the life of our churches as they grow in unity.

Christ is the sole source of authority. The exercise of authority in the church is an act of service; service of the Word, revealed and witnessed in the Scriptures and service of the Kingdom of God and his Christ. The structures and styles of authority in the churches are closely related to their understandings of their ministry and their worship, and, indeed, of themselves as churches. The churches must therefore be sensitive to what is regarded as essential by some and not by others.

Ecumenical instruments should work within the existing patterns and structures of church authority. They should serve the churches by enabling them to grow together into unity and to act together in such areas as evangelism, worship and social responsibility. The instruments should have simple, flexible structures, which are adaptable to serve the growth and changing needs of the Church as it seeks to do God's will. At the national level the instruments must make it possible for those who speak for the churches to speak together and with authority to government and nation. They should provide a means by which we can talk not only to one another but to those of other faiths and those of none. The ecumenical instruments can help to create a climate in which we can openly and trustingly explore our differences.

Councils of Churches at all levels should be a real sign of our unity of mind, heart, will and action with Christ. They should seek to undertake specific tasks, sharing their personal and financial resources generously to the common endeavour.

Mission and service

Our task as the Body of Christ is to go out in love with the whole gospel for the whole world. We are challenged both to share the good news by our words and also to *be* the Good News by our life and actions, as we respond to the call to holiness.

We believe that Christian faith is of its very nature missionary – concerned to share its truth and life with the contemporary world. Mission embraces explicit evangelism – that proclamation of the gospel which seeks to evoke a personal response of commitment to Christ and his Church; sacrificial service to God's world with all its needs and potential; struggle for justice in the face of inequality and oppression.

Priorities in our mission include both tasks within the Christian community and outreach to others. These involve building up the people of God by educating and training both clergy and laity at all ages and stages of development; by rooting our lives in prayer and the scriptures and by developing an awareness of God at the heart of our common life and service; by living according to the gospel, in community, as a sign of fulfilment or contradiction in what so often seems a materialistic, privatised and idolatrous society; by discerning and using the gifts of all in new and perhaps surprising ways.

Another requirement is listening and learning with humility by turning from past arrogance to receive from our fellow Christians and also from those of other faiths and none; by recognising and celebrating the community of black and white, young and old, male and female, lay and ordained; by daring to love and be loved, to serve and be served by those who seem different or unlovely.

Outreach includes sharing the Gospel with those, in Britain and beyond, in urban and rural areas, who are powerless, oppressed and often alienated by the Churches; with those, in Britain and beyond, who are complacent, rich or powerful and who must hear God's word of challenge to them spoken boldly; with those we encounter in daily life whose lives may be empty or who long for a more inspiring and sustaining meaning to their work and life, and who have yet to hear Christians giving reasons for the hope that is in them.

Working together

We are called to do justly, to love mercy and to walk humbly with God and with each other.

Identified priorities in mission should be shared, for mission and unity are ultimately indivisible. Much is already and effectively shared; but so much more remains to be done. The churches' people and resources are gifts for the building up of the Kingdom. Duplication and dissipation of these are to be avoided. We are not necessarily called to pool our resources: another pattern is to allow one church or agency to act on behalf of others. There are ways of co-operation without amalgamation. We are called to trust one another and to take "holy risks" for the sake of common mission. Competitive evangelism is no longer acceptable, and on every agenda the first question should be "is this a priority?" and the second "how can we do this together?"

We recognise that God is calling us to work together much more closely in four major areas:

Work for, with, and by young people

It is difficult to overestimate the value of involvement in Greenbelt, Iona, Taize, ecumenical work camps, events organised by Scripture Union, British Youth for Christ, etc. Similar experiences need to be available at more local level.

Caring service in partnership with the State, and with voluntary and statutory agencies

Examples suggested are care for people with AIDS, care of the elderly and the dying, housing associations and hostels for the homeless, work with refugees, counselling centres, the alleviation of poverty, world development, hospitals, prisons, industry, commerce, the armed services and education.

Nurture and training

There is also a need to enable ecumenical nurture and training of both lay and ordained, though we recognise that substantial theological differences of understanding cannot and should not be overlooked. Lent '86 showed that diversity of belief and practice can be seen as enriching rather than threatening. Formation for the ordained ministry and post-ordination training should be strongly ecumenical and further schemes of joint training should be encouraged. This would help those who have pastoral responsibility confidently to encourage ecumenical contacts between the congregations they serve. Local clergy, ministers and lay leaders have an influential role for promoting or hindering Christian unity. Opportunities afforded by the growing emphasis on specialist training of lay-leaders should also be seized.

Church and society

At the interface between church and world we recognise how much we need each other to affirm what is good and challenge what is bad in today's society. We need to take the exciting opportunities opened up by the revolution in communication. Not every political issue will produce a common Christian response. But there are few social problems today to which there are specifically denominational approaches. We have much hard thinking to do together on moral issues. We are called to demonstrate how we can live in growing and deepening Christian fellowship while holding different views on many important issues. While dealing sensitively with the great biblical themes of justice and peace, we must not stifle the prophetic voice, such as the condemnation of racism which the world is hearing increasingly *from* the churches, and which is addressed also *to* the churches, calling us to tackle racism and other forms of prejudice evident within our church life.

In our continuing pilgrimage of sharing we note as examples:

- prayer, worship and study together;
- rationalisation of buildings and other resources;
- the development of more local ecumenical projects, local covenants and covenants of church leaders;
- preparation and support for marriage and pastoral concern for interchurch families;
- local ecumenical learning;
- true partnership with Christians from other parts of the world "seeing ourselves as others see us".

In all of these ways, practical and visionary, we should strive for achievable goals, working at appropriate levels, and seeking to retain a spirit of graciousness and invitation rather than coercion. We recommend undertaking an "ecumenical audit" of resources and potential to ascertain in any given situation what can be done together now.

5 MEMBERSHIP

1   The new ecumenical bodies will have several distinct categories of membership. At the inauguration of the new ecumenical bodies, all those churches participating in the Not Strangers but Pilgrims Inter-Church Process (see p.105) may become members in the appropriate categories as may be agreed by the Inter-Church Meeting. After the 1990 inauguration of the new ecumenical bodies, applications for each category of membership will need to be agreed by 75% of the existing full members as defined below in paragraph 2.

2   (a) Full membership is open to those churches or associations of local churches within one Christian tradition which accept the Basis and Commitment of the new ecumenical bodies, which also have a spread of congregations in one or more of the four nations, and which have their own national organisation and ecclesial identity.

(b) A church, which on principle has no credal statements in its tradition and therefore cannot formally subscribe to the statement of faith in the Basis, may nevertheless apply for and be elected to full membership provided that it satisfies those members churches which subscribe to the Basis that it manifests faith in Christ as witnessed to in the Scriptures and is committed to the aims and purposes of the new ecumenical body, and that it will work in the spirit of the Basis.

3   Bodies (associations, networks, movements, etc.) which bring together Christians of different denominations for purposes congruent with the Basis and Aims of the new ecumenical body may be received into the status of "bodies in association", or, in Scotland, "participant members" (see p.51), with one or more of the new ecumenical bodies. They will be bodies with a spread of member groups and an appropriate form of national organisation in at least one of the four nations. A specific number of places will be agreed for representatives of such "bodies in association" in the Assembly and equivalent gatherings. Representatives of these bodies may speak and vote on all matters save amendment of the Constitution. These bodies will be expected to pay an appropriate annual membership fee and will be invited to share fully in the working groups, networks, and commissions of the new ecumenical bodies.

4   Associate membership is available for churches or associations of churches which are eligible for membership but are not ready to take up the full duties and privileges of membership. Representatives of associate members may

speak but not vote. Associate members shall be expected to make a financial contribution of approximately half that for full members.

5   Observer status is a matter for consideration and decision by each new ecumenical body separately.

6 PARTICIPATION AND REPRESENTATION

1   These are themes which are closely related and arise in all discussions about church organisation. We do not see perfect solutions. But we are aware of the issues and would point towards the way of facing them in our ecumenical work.

2   It was an outstanding feature of the 1986 Lent groups that participation was extensive and active. In the ecumenical future the same widespread enthusiasm will be needed, and the formal structures will be called to listen carefully to what is expressed by local groups of Christians. Councils of Churches, or their equivalent, at local and intermediate levels will encourage local ecumenical house groups and prayer groups, not only in Lent, but as a normal part of church life. Christians participate in the whole ecumenical movement as they build bridges between churches in the locality.

3   The desirability of widespread consultation about an issue is another aspect of participation. We would encourage the new ecumenical bodies to use the facilities offered by the media to seek response to major possibilities of joint action, so that there is widespread discussion.

4   People participate also as they represent a local church in the national gathering of their denomination. All churches are becoming aware of the need to ensure a good balance in such representation, and it is only as the churches give effect to such balance that representative ecumenical meetings can reflect the character of the whole people of God.

5   In the new ecumenical bodies each church has places allocated for its representatives. In certain cases the possibility of broader representation is limited, for example if national senior representatives are to be brought together. But where there is no such limitation, the tendency may still be to send only senior clergy and ministers. Experience teaches us that there is much to be gained in ecumenical meetings and gatherings where there is a community of women and men, ordained and lay, black and white, young, middle-aged and old, as well as a theological and geographical spread.

6   It is therefore of vital importance where, in these new ecumenical bodies, places are allocated to churches and there is more than one place per church, that each church should ensure a balance in its delegation which will contribute to the balance of the whole.

7 ASSEMBLIES AND NATIONAL MEETINGS

Throughout this continuing inter-church pilgrimage, authority rests with the decision-making bodies of the member churches. It is therefore important that a considerable number of people who represent their churches on the British and Irish Assembly, and on the equivalent national gatherings, should be members of their own church's decision-making body. The timing of meetings of the Assembly and of the national gatherings will be important, so that they can be constructively related to the decision-making gatherings of the member churches. These meetings also need to be integrated into a coherent and manageable pattern among themselves. We therefore propose initially that meetings of the British and Irish Assembly be held every other year, alternating with meetings of the equivalent national gatherings. In this way many of the same people will meet every year — one year with representatives of churches from all the nations, and the other year with representatives of churches in their own nation only. It will be open to the member churches to propose additional meetings in due course.

8 MAJOR GATHERINGS

1   The Inter-Church Process provides an opportunity to envisage the organisation of large, media-aware gatherings. Although many Christians in these islands have been inspired by attending such events as the German Kirchentag, it is plain that the context must determine the particular style of event, and no imitation is possible. In this section the churches are offered suggestions, not firm proposals.

2   The aims of major gatherings may be listed as

    – to enable many Christians to meet, to worship, study, pray, discuss together, and so to experience the breadth of the church in these islands;

    – to provide a major witness to the Gospel which will engage the interest of the media and influence the moral and spiritual awareness of the nations;

    – to offer an opportunity for British and Irish Christians to hear outstanding leaders and teachers of the worldwide Church;

    – to be a sign and celebration of our growing unity in Christ.

3   In order that the churches may build on their experience, we suggest that the first post-1990 major gatherings be in each of the four nations, or, in the case of England, nationally or regionally, and that a gathering for Britain and Ireland be attempted only after that. We do not set down any timetable at this stage.

4   Organisation of such events is complex, and although voluntary help may enable a great deal to be done it will probably not be adequate for everything. The organising committee for each major event will need both freedom to plan and good links with the new ecumenical bodies and the Churches. We therefore suggest that each of the new ecumenical bodies write in a budget figure for Major Gatherings which can accumulate until an organising committee is in being, and then may be placed at its disposal.

5   It is hoped that there might be a relationship between future Lent study courses and major gatherings, so that as many people as possible may have some active participation.

9 FINANCING THE NEW BODIES

Churches participating in the inter-church pilgrimage will express their new commitment by a readiness to use all their resources in ways which progressively involve common planning and action (see Introduction p.3 above). For example, a staff member may be undertaking work for all the churches for a period, or one church may be hosting a consultation for all. Whatever the calls of this sort made from time to time, a regular financial contribution to the budget of the new ecumenical bodies will also be needed.

The main financial principles which are presented at the start of the new ecumenical bodies are as follows:

a   That every participating church will make a regular financial contribution, which is evidence of commitment to our growing unity.

b   The regular askings for the budget for the coordinating and representative work of the new ecumenical bodies will be brought together, so that each church knows both its overall figure and how that will be divided.

c   The asking will be presented to the churches for each three year period and will be amended only for inflation (including the movement of wages) and for emergencies, so that there is not an annual debate regarding contribution.

d   Each of the new ecumenical bodies will have a measure of flexibility to shift resources internally and may, if its representative bodies approve, request supplementary help from sources other than member churches, without either prejudicing the apportionment of the churches' annual contributions or placing on the churches claims for additional support.

NOTES

1   Since many churches have budgeted support for Councils of Churches over many years, the figure they have accepted for 1990 is the starting point for consideration over the following period.

2   It is possible to consider various indices for fixing contributions, none being without difficulty e.g. by membership or by total income, or by size of representation on conciliar assemblies. It is recommended that these and other possibilities be discussed by the new ecumenical bodies during the years 1991-3.

3   For the period 1991/2/3 (calendar years) the churches already in membership of existing councils are requested to accept an overall contribution to the new ecumenical bodies as being their 1990 figure adjusted each year in the light of inflation.

4   Those churches which have not hitherto made such provision are asked to discuss with the officers of the Inter-Church Meeting what would be an appropriate contribution in the first years of the new ecumenical bodies.

5   For the three-year initial period 1991/2/3 the minimum figure of total annual contribution to the new ecumenical bodies will normally be £500 where two or more of them are involved and £250 where one only is involved. The officers of the new ecumenical bodies will act in situations where all requirements of membership are met but there is inability to meet these minimum figures.

6   It will be the responsibility of the appropriate officers of the new ecumenical bodies (these will normally include Treasurers and General Secretaries) to bring together their proposed budgets so that, every three years, there may be a discussion of the proper distribution of the contributions income. This may vary over the years as the work develops and emphases change. The General Secretaries of the new ecumenical bodies will prepare a joint proposal. This will be submitted to the appropriate authorities in the new ecumenical bodies for their consideration and approval. If approved by all, the figures will be sent to the churches as the request for the next three year period. If not so approved it will be for the Church Representatives' Meeting of the Council of Churches for Britain and Ireland (which is the point at which all the churches are presesnt through their senior representatives) to consider the points at issue and seek an acceptable solution which may be then sent to the churches.

7   The Council of Churches for Britain and Ireland will endeavour to bring together the record of annual church contributions and their distribution, so that the churches have an annual account, in simplified form, of what has been raised and how it has been apportioned. This will include, as far as possible, amounts raised for those agencies constitutionally related to the new ecumenical bodies and any other contributions authorised by the new ecumenical bodies.

8   The churches will be responsible for the expenses of their representatives to assemblies of the new ecumenical bodies. The expenses of committee members will be a matter for each ecumenical body to decide, for the decision will depend on the role of the member and the frequency of the meetings and whether the churches or the ecumenical body make the appointment.

9   It is expected that, with the agreement of its member churches, following the inauguration of the new ecumenical bodies, the British Council of Churches will transfer income and capital as appropriate to the new bodies.

10 ENGLAND

1 Introduction

The Swanwick Conference of 1987 said, "Ecumenical instruments should serve the churches by enabling them to grow together in unity and to act together in such areas as evangelism, worship and social responsibility."

We are grateful for the ninety-one responses received which we have carefully considered. It has to be said that many were contradictory. In the light of these we have produced proposals which are as modest as we think possible consonant with the Swanwick vision.

Here we set these out as the way by which churches in England may be supported and resourced as they "grow together" and "act together" at national, intermediate and local levels.

England has never had a national Council of Churches as its neighbours have. However, it has developed a number of ecumenical bodies at other levels and the Ecumenical Officer for England of the British Council of Churches has supported and encouraged inter-church co-operation at all levels. These proposals reflect both continuity and newness.

The body will be known as CHURCHES TOGETHER IN ENGLAND, a new title which reflects the new life-style of ecumenical relationships of the churches in England. The Working Party considered a very wide range of possible names and finally decided on this one.

They did not believe the word "commission" was a suitable description for the instrument being proposed. They had difficulties also with "council", "congress", "synod", "assembly", all of which have technical usages in the churches which were not suitable for this new form of ecumenical instrument.

The use of the word "English" was discarded in favour of "in England" in order to reflect the fact that a number of the expected member churches do not have their origins in England but are located there, whilst others cover a wider geographical area than England alone.

2 Basis and Commitment

Churches Together in England unites in pilgrimage those churches in England which, acknowledging God's revelation in Christ, confess the Lord Jesus Christ as God and Saviour according to the Scriptures; and, in obedience to God's will and in the power of the Holy Spirit commit themselves to seek a deepening of their communion with Christ and with one another in the Church, which is his body, and

to fulfil their mission to proclaim the Gospel by common witness and service in the world,

to the glory of the one God, Father, Son and Holy Spirit.

3 Aims and Functions

The aims and functions of Churches Together in England have been developed and adapted from those in the Swanwick Report and are as follows:

To be a visible sign of the churches' commitment to one another, in obedience to our Lord's prayer "that all of them may be one, Father, just as you are in me and I am in you; may they also be in us so that the world may believe that you have sent me". (John 17.21) (NIV).

To promote the theological reflection necessary to support the ecumenical movement and to enable continuing discussion of Faith and Order issues, especially of the nature and purpose and unity of the Church in the light of its mission.

To encourage shared worship and prayer, learning, service and evangelism, with each church sharing with others the treasures of its tradition.

To enable the churches to develop growing and changing relationships, as pilgrims, together, in the living and sharing of the gospel, and to facilitate further steps towards fuller unity in England, including consideration of theological and practical questions, especially those arising from local ecumenical projects.

To enable the churches, as they grow together in unity, to seek a common mind and to share decision-making in common.

To enable the churches to respond to the needs of society at all levels, to explore church and society issues within the English conext and, when appropriate, to make approaches to secular authorities independently or with others.

To promote, co-ordinate, support and service intermediate bodies in England, assisting them in their care for local ecumenical activity and representing their concerns at the national level.

To seek to ensure that the departments, divisions and boards of the churches at national and intermediate levels work together as closely as possible so that their work may be co-ordinated.

To promote the appointment and support of full- or part-time ecumenical officers or their equivalents at the intermediate level throughout England.

To encourage the review of ecclesiastical boundaries in England so that they may be aligned as closely as possible with each other and with the civil boundaries in order to promote the shared mission of the churches.

4 Ecumenical Relations (at local, intermediate and national levels in England)

Local

An outstanding feature of local ecumenism in England is its rich diversity. Prayer groups, community care, evangelistic exercises, and much more are to be found in many places. Many of these activities are relatively informal and have only the minimum of structure. It is from this kind of activity that a deeper, more permanent commitment is growing among Christians. It is in this fertile soil that local ecumenical projects including local covenants are rooted.

One of the aims of Churches Together in England is to affirm, support and service local ecumenism whether it be formal or informal, structured or unstructured. In this it reflects the concerns of the Swanwick Report which said, "There is a heartfelt desire for this local dimension to be affirmed and continued; and for resources to be identified in order that lay Christians may be equipped to share their faith in the secular world with those of other faiths and those of none."

In its supportive role Churches Together in England will be concerned to service the following formal structures which have been developing over many years.

Local councils of churches. These vary in size from three to over one hundred member bodies, and provide a forum, a mouthpiece and a tool for inter-church co-operation. They are autonomous bodies and vary not only in size but in effectiveness, and they attempt to enable their member churches to relate to issues affecting their own locality. Many associate with the British Council of Churches while a number are related more closely to the large councils of churches covering a metropolitan area or a county.

In many parts of England there exist local Free Church Councils which are a further expression of churches sharing together. Over recent years a number have moved into closer relationship with local councils of churches either as a department or a committee or by total absorption.

The BCC service to local councils of churches has been to provide the quarterly publication, Vision One, and the advice and specialised input available from its staff. Local councils of churches have looked to the BCC for help in constitutional matters such as the constitution itself, or whether or not to admit a particular body to full or associate membership. They are often the channel by which the BCC has been able to service local congregations in such matters as, for example, Christian Aid, Keep Sunday Special, race relations, peace issues and so forth. They provided much of the organisation for study groups in Lent '86.

How may these be serviced in the future? The following proposals for future structures will still enable local councils of churches to call on the advice and help of people with wider experience of councils of churches and of the churches generally. It is suggested that local councils of churches at present related to an "umbrella" council such as Birmingham or Cleveland or Merseyside should continue to do so. Where no such relationship exists it is recommended that they relate to the ecumenical council or sponsoring body for their area (see below). The subscription they currently pay the BCC (in 1988 £3 per member congregation per annum) would then be paid to the ecumenical council or sponsoring body for their area, and this would go some way towards providing support at the intermediate level. There are proposals in this report for personnel at both the intermediate level and for the north and south of England.

Local ecumenical projects (LEPs) The experience of commitment gained in LEPs has contributed towards the climate which has enabled the Inter-Church Process to develop in England. LEPs, of which there are now about 550, exist at the level of the local church where relationships have moved on from the co-operation of a council of churches to a formal, written agreement making it possible for Christians of more than one denomination to share buildings or congregational life or sacramental ministry or a combination of all three in a closely committed way, founded on mutual trust, and approved by their respective church authorities. Into this category also come local covenants where separate buildings and church life continue denominationally but a commitment is made to do everything together that conscience will permit and to do separately only what cannot be done together. LEPs are pioneering at the boundaries of ecumenical relations and so need support and reassurance from their parent denominations.

Currently they are serviced by sponsoring bodies (see below) and by the

Consultative Committee for Local Ecumenical Projects in England (CCLEPE). It is not suggested that there should be any change in these arrangements. The work of CCLEPE will be continued within Churches Together in England.

Intermediate

In England the churches have developed a network of ecumenical bodies which serve them at an intermediate level. Ecumenical relations in England have therefore to be seen as the sum of the local, intermediate and national expressions of Christian sharing.

The intermediate bodies, sometimes called ecumenical councils, sometimes sponsoring bodies, sometimes church leaders' meetings, have worked out useful ways of covering various areas of work.

Sponsoring Bodies provide pastoral care and supervision for LEPs on behalf of the churches. Examples may be found in Dorset, South Yorkshire, Derbyshire, and Somerset and South Avon.

Ecumenical councils and **metropolitan councils of churches** are ecumenical bodies whose agenda include evangelism, church formation, adult Christian education, youth work, social responsibility, industrial mission, ministerial training, world development and overseas aid, ecumenical affairs and communication. Some, like Birmingham Council of Christian Churches, Merseyside and Region Churches Ecumenical Assembly, or Greater Manchester County Ecumenical Council divide their work into specialist sub-groups. Greater Bristol Ecumenical Council acts as the enabler for its member churches to work ecumenically. Cleveland Council of Churches and Sheffield Council of Churches provide a forum for representatives of their member churches to meet and address issues of church and society.

Birmingham, Merseyside, Manchester, Milton Keynes, Lincolnshire, Telford and West Yorkshire employ full-time executive officers. Bristol, Cleveland, Cumbria, Hertfordshire and Bedfordshire, Kent, and Lichfield Diocesan Area Liaison group employ half-time paid officers. In Cumbria the post is combined with that of the churches' Radio Officer.

Church leaders' meetings. Church leaders (by which is meant those in leadership as senior representative officers of the churches), meet regularly. They share together their understanding of church life within their constituencies and in some cases have developed a common approach to mission in their area. In East London, Lancashire, Lincolnshire, and Merseyside, church leaders have made covenants together. Where church leaders have covenanted, signifying their commitment to one another, this is a visible sign to their churches of their own ecumenical priorities, as well as an encouragement to congregations to enter into covenanted relationships. It is hoped that successors will sign the covenant.

Ecumenical officers. Before examining the role of ecumenical officers it is important to recognise that ecumenical development throughout England is not uniform nor is it expected to be. Ecumenical bodies vary in size, structure and agenda. They will continue to do so.

If sharing between local churches is to be adequately supported there needs to be at the intermediate level a strong ecumenical body to provide that support. Employing an ecumenical officer whose expertise and time are available to local churches and to church leaders is one means of ensuring that the intermediate bodies can fulfil their role more effectively. This lay behind the Swanwick proposal for ecumenically appointed ecumenical officers, "full-time if possible".

At present there are ten full-time, ecumenically appointed ecumenical officers or executive secretaries of ecumenical councils. Each is a key person in their own area. They are in Birmingham, Cumbria, Lancashire, Lincolnshire, Manchester, Merseyside, Milton Keynes, Telford and West Yorkshire. All are in the midlands and the north.

It is clear that resources will not be possible in every case for a county to have its own full-time, paid ecumenical officer. In some situations, such as Telford, for instance, the circumstances require a full-time officer appointed by the churches together to serve an area smaller than a county.

Some of the work of the ecumenical officer is advisory, giving counsel to church leaders or to LEPs or to committees on inter-church and Faith and Order matters. Some of their work is pastoral, providing support to clergy and ministers, enabling officers of local councils of churches, encouraging people in LEPs or local covenants who are trying to make sense of church rules in areas of uncertainty. Sometimes they have to handle correspondence or covenants and sharing agreements, or be the go-between on behalf of the churches, or be secretary of a sponsoring body or ecumenical council with all the attendant "office" work. Some of them deal with social responsibility and youth work and are aware of the agenda of the churches in specialist areas. It is clear that in the future their role will take on a greater significance as the churches seek to initiate, affirm, and support local ecumenical activity.

The Field Officers of Churches Together in England will continue the work currently done by the Ecumenical Officer for England in liaising with and resourcing these intermediate bodies and their officers.

The appointment of denominational ecumenical officers at intermediate level has been a crucial factor in response to a real need. Sometimes they work as a team for their area.

5 The Forum

I Purpose

A Forum will be established whose purpose will be to provide an opportunity for people representing the churches at local, intermediate and national level to meet.

II Functions

The Forum will be the "eyes and ears" of the churches. It will meet to worship, share and listen, and have the following functions:

a   to recommend to the churches such matters as it believes should be addressed jointly.

b   to support and encourage intermediate bodies in their role as the servants of their participating churches especially in the area of promoting local ecumenism.

c   to share its reflections on the activities and future programmes of the Enabling Group, Co-ordinating Groups and Agencies of Churches Together in England in the fulfilment of thier role of servicing the churches.

d   to elect: its Moderator and Deputy Moderator and other members directly elected from it to the Enabling Group (as described in Section 6 (II) on membership of the Enabling Group) and such other appointments as may be necessary.

III Representation

The Forum will comprise about 360 participants who will be appointed from three categories: (a) **national** comprising about ½ of its membership; (b) **intermediate** comprising about ⅓ of its membership; (c) **others** comprising about ⅙th of its membership. It is hoped that the participants in the Forum will be as representative as possible. Attention is drawn to the importance of the statements made in the common section on Participation (see page 19). Allocations of places will be kept under review in consultation with the Enabling Group.

a   National

(i)   Churches and associations of churches of one Christian Tradition.

The number of places on the forum allocated to each church recognises the membership and/or attendance figures for each church or Association of churches. The figures presented below may need revision in the light of comments received.

It is hoped that there will be equal numbers of ordained and lay people. To enable this to happen the number of participants in this category is in multiples of two.

All churches having six or more places should allocate one-sixth of those places to those who are between the ages of 18 and 30.

The following allocation of places is proposed. It is hoped that other churches and associations of churches who have not yet been involved in Inter-Church Process may be actively encouraged to participate fully in Churches Together in England.

The figures favour the smaller member churches recognising that the larger ones will probably be predominant in the representation from the intermediate bodies.

It is assumed that those participating in the Inter-church Process will wish to become members of CTE. The places will be distributed as follows:

African Methodist Episcopal Church	2
Baptist Union of Great Britain	12
Calvary Church of God in Christ	2
Cherubim and Seraphim	2
Christian Brethren	6
Church of England	36
Church of Scotland (Presbytery of England)	2
Congregational Federation	2
Greek Orthodox	6
Independent Methodists	2
Lutheran Council of Great Britain	2
Methodist Church	18
Moravian Church	2
New Testament Assembly	2
Oriental Orthodox	2

Religious Society of Friends	4
Roman Catholic	32
Russian Orthodox	2
Salvation Army	6
Shiloh United Church of Christ	2
United Reformed Church	12
Wesleyan Holiness Church	2
Total	158

NB the figure of 158 may rise as other churches and associations of churches seek membership.

(ii) Federations of churches/associations of churches.

Nationally established bodies which represent churches and associations of churches of more than one Christian tradition shall be eligible for membership. Where such bodies include churches and associations of churches who are already directly represented on the Forum it is hoped that such federations may nominate as participants to the Forum representatives from churches not directly in membership.

Each member in this category will be entitled to 2 places.

Currently these are:
Afro West Indian United Council of Churches
Black Pastor's Conference
Council of African and Afro Caribbean Churches
Free Church Federal Council
International Ministerial Council of Great Britain
West Indian Evangelical Alliance

(iii) Associate Members (see Section 5, para. 5, p. 18 above)

Where applications are approved each Associate Member will be entitled to 2 places on the Forum.

b   Intermediate Bodies

There will be about 120 places on the Forum for representatives of the churches at local and intermediate levels. There are 44 sponsoring bodies/ecumenical councils or equivalents, each of which will initially be entitled to two places except in the case of larger conurbations.

The suggested allocation of places is as follows:

NORTH EAST
Cleveland Council of Churches	2
Durham Ecumenical Relations Group	2

Newcastle Church Relations Group

YORKSHIRE AND HUMBERSIDE

Leeds Metropolitan Council of Churches	2
Sheffield Council of Churches	2
South Cleveland & N. Yorks. Ecumenical Council	2
South Yorkshire Ecumenical Sponsoring Group	2
Humberside Churches Council	2
West Yorkshire Ecumenical Council	2

NORTH WEST

Cheshire Church Leaders Group	2
Cumbria Sponsoring Body	2
Greater Manchester County Ecumenical Council	4
Lancashire Sponsoring Body	2
Merseyside and Region Churches Ecumenical Assembly	4

WEST MIDLANDS

Birmingham Council of Christian Churches	4
Coventry and Warwickshire Ecumenical Council	2
Hereford County Sponsoring Body	2
Lichfield Diocesan Area Liaison Group	2
Telford Christian Council	2
Worcestershire County Sponsoring Body	2

EAST MIDLANDS

Derbyshire Sponsoring Body	2
Leicestershire Diocesan Area Sponsoring Body	2
Lincolnshire and South Humberside Sponsoring Body	2
Northamptonshire Ecumenical Council	2
Nottinghamshire Ecumenical Council	2

EAST ANGLIA

Cambridge Ecumenical Council	2
Norfolk Ecumenical Council	2
Suffolk Ecumenical Council	2

SOUTH EAST (North)

Berkshire Ecumenical Council	2
Buckinghamshire Ecumenical Council	2
Essex Churches Consultative Committee	2
Hertfordshire and Bedfordshire Ecumenical Commitee	2
Milton Keynes Christian Council	2
Oxfordshire Ecumenical Council	2

SOUTH EAST (South)

Hampshire and the Islands Ecumenical Council	2
Kent Ecumenical Council	2
Surrey Sponsoring Body	2
Sussex Sponsoring Body	2

LONDON

Barking Area Church Leaders' Group	2
East London Church Leaders' Group	2
North London Church Leaders' Group	2
South London Church Leaders' Group	4
West London Church Leaders' Group	2

SOUTH WEST

Cornwall Church Leaders' Group	2
Devon	2
Dorset Sponsoring Body	2
Gloucestershire Sponsoring Body	2
Greater Bristol Ecumenical Council	2
Somerset and South Avon Sponsoring Body	2
Wiltshire Sponsoring Body	2

ISLAND COUNCILS

Guernsey Council of Churches	2
Isle of Man Council of Churches	2
Jersey Council of Churches	2

As far as possible one person should be concerne with church strategy in the area and one represent local councils of churches. But see also the recommendations on Participation (page 19).

Elections will be arranged by the ecumenical council or sponsoring body in consultation with councils of churches in their area. This could be carried out at an intermediate gathering or other meeting together.

A subscription per place per annum would be payable to cover the costs of a bi-ennial residential Forum and meetings of the Enabling Group, and would also cover the cost of travel on a fares-pool basis. At 1990 prices this is expected to be £80 per place.

c   **Other.** This will cover a variety of groupings listed below and will total approximately 50.

Ex Officio 10

Youth Participants. Appointments arranged by the
English Churches Youth Services   10

Co-ordinating Groups and any permanent **Agencies**
set up by the Churches for England   Up to 15

Bodies in Association Elected by such bodies in
consultation with the Enabling Group   6

Co-options Nominated by the Enabling Group   8

Representatives from other bodies
Council of Churches for Britain and Ireland   1
General Secretary, COCBI   1
CYTUN (Council of Churches for Wales)   1
ACTS (Action of Churches Together in Scotland)   1
Irish Inter-Church Meeting ("Ballymascanlon")   1
General Secretary, Free Church Federal Council   1

d Observers

The member churches and associations of churches comprising Churches
Together in England may invite churches, and associations of churches of
one Christian tradition for whom Full or Associate Membership may be
inappropriate to appoint one observer to participate in the Forum. Such
Observers will not be entitled to vote, but may speak at the discretion of the
Moderator/Deputy Moderator.

IV Meetings

The Forum will meet every two years over a long week-end.

Since it will only meet every two years and the dates are fixed will in advance
it is hoped that there will be strong lay representation. Churches are encouraged
to find ways to reimburse lay representatives who may have to take unpaid leave
to attend the Forum and/or the Enabling Group.

The style of the meetings will lay stress on: working in small groups; the
possibility of sub-sections of the Forum to reflect upon major issues; the
opportunity for the different churches, and the intermediate bodies to meet.
All this will be within the context of worship which was so enriching at
Swanwick.

V Ex Officio Members of the Forum and the Enabling Group

A Moderator and Deputy Moderator of the Forum

(i)   They will be elected by the Forum for a period of four years, one being
a lay person and one being ordained.

(ii) They will preside at sessions of the Forum and prepare its agenda with the General Secretary following consultation with the Enabling Group.

(iii) They will be aware of all aspects of the work of Churches Together in England.

Honorary Treasurer

He/she will normally be a lay person with financial expertise coupled with proved commitment to the ecumenical cause. The appointment will be made by the Enabling Group for four years and he/she will serve on the Enabling Group and the Forum.

General Secretary and Other Executive Staff

The General Secretary will serve both Enabling Group and Forum. In addition there will be three other executive staff members (as defined in section 9 below).

Convenor and Deputy Convenor of the Enabling Group

(i) They will be elected by the Enabling Group at their first meeting which will take place during the Forum and will serve until the next Forum. The appointment is renewable for two subsequent terms. One will be ordained and the other lay.

(ii) They will be responsible for chairing the Enabling Group and preparing the agenda for meetings along with the General Secretary.

A Chaplain

In addition there will be a Chaplain who will be responsible for planning and arranging worship at meetings of the Forum and the Enabling Group. This will be a role of encouraging and facilitating others to participate.

He/she may develop a pastoral role in relation to the staff of Churches Together in England, in particular acting as an independent source of support.

He/she will normally be ordained and will be appointed by the Enabling Group for a term of office of two years, renewable for a further two years, and will serve both it and the Forum.

VI A Process

The Forum will be seen as part of a continuing process of prayer, reflection and growth. Thus:

a. Forum participants will be kept in touch with the life and work of CTE by the Secretariat.

b. Participants should be appointed at least nine months ahead of a Forum so that they can take part in any preparatory meetings and receive appropriate mailings.

c. In order that continuity and enthusiasm be maintained, participants will be encouraged to meet between Forum meetings in groups, such as: regional meetings of intermediate bodies, and national meetings (for example: participants from one church, and young people).

6 The Enabling Group

I Functions

The Enabling Group will be a reference point partly serving the Forum and partly enabling the churches to make decisions in common. It will respond to initiatives from the churches and will not so much carry out policy as enable the initiatives to be carried out by the churches in consultation with each other, often through co-ordinating groups or agencies established by the churches.

II Membership

Recognising that the Forum will meet only bi-ennially the Enabling Group will be a large enough body to represent a wide spectrum of church life. All members of the Enabling Group will be participants in the Form. They will be drawn from 4 categories: National (15); Intermediate Bodies (10); elected by the Forum (12); Ex Officio (12). Initially the total membership will be 49.

(a) National: These will be appointed by the appropriate authorities within the following churches and associations of churches from those who have direct access to the decision-making structures of their churches:

Church of England	3
Roman Catholic	3
Methodist	2
Baptist	1
United Reformed	1

The following will be appointed by the participating bodies in the Forum representing the categories listed below:

Other churches in England in membership of the FCFC	1
Black-led churches	2
Other member churches	2

(b) Intermediate Bodies: Elected via regional groupings (see listing on pp. 35-7) 10

(c) **Elected by the Forum:** At least 4 of whom
are aged between 18-30   12

(d) **Ex Officio:** Moderator and Deputy Moderator
of the Forum   2
Honorary Treasurer, General Secretary   2
Executive Staff   3
General Secretary of COCBI   1
General Secretary of Free Church Federal Council   1
Convenor and Deputy Convenor   2
Chaplain   1

III Meetings

Careful consideration will need to be given to both style and frequency of the Enabling Group's meetings and some, at least, of these will be residential. At least three meetings per year will be necessary to have continuity of reflection and to build relationships between members.

The Enabling Group may invite consultants (members of Co-ordinating Groups, Agencies or individuals with expertise) to attend its meetings.

IV Casual Vacancies

The Enabling Group will, after appropriate consultation, be responsible for filling casual vacancies.

7 Co-ordinating Groups

Certain areas of work will be done through CHURCHES' CO-ORDINATING GROUPS.

Currently, there are some groups bringing together people with similar responsibilities within the churches e.g. Home Mission/Evangelism Secretaries, Youth Officers. They pray together and compare methods of working and programmes. They decide what can be done jointly, what one church can do on behalf of the rest and what can be applied from one church's experience to current initiatives in other churches. They provide models for churches' Co-ordinating Groups.

This style of inter-church co-operation will be encurged in a variety of programmes within the churches (see below). This will involve affirming some Groups already in existence, challenging the working pattern of others and considering the setting up of Groups where nothing similar to a Co-ordinating Group is in existence.

These Groups would vary in size, frequency of meeting and length of life. They will mainly be drawn from people in the churches whose specific task is to work in the area of concern.

Recognising the need for complementary agenda in some areas of work it may be desirable or necessary to work with the Council of Churches for Britain and Ireland or other national bodies, especially with Cytun (Churches Together in Wales) because of the legislation common to England and Wales, for example, in the fields of social responsibility and education (Churches Joint Education Policy Committee already serves England and Wales).

It is proposed that the work of the **Consultative Committee for Local Ecumenical Projects in England (CCLEPE)** will be continued by a **Local Ecumenical Development Advisory Group (LEDAG),** with the addition of responsibilities for care for local councils of churches and ecumenical officers, matters of liturgy and worship affecting local ecumenism, and acting as a clearing house for information concerning the sale and sharing of church buildings. Initially the membership of this group should follow the same criteria as that of CCLEPE. Thereafter the basis of membership will be reviewed.

It is proposed that the Co-ordinating Groups will continue work already being undertaken in England in the areas of mission and evangelism (including Partnership in Evangelism), youth services and church and society issues within the English context.

As envisaged in the Swanwick Report (p. 18) a Co-ordinating Group will be established for Faith and Order matters to deal with practical and theological issues on the way to fuller Christian unity in England.

It will be necessary to explore with the churches, COCBI and the intermediate bodies how best to co-ordinate the concerns of industrial mission, Christian education, adult formation and ministries.

Churches Together in England will need to consider if Co-ordinating Groups are needed for the promotion of prayer, and for worship and liturgy, and it will need to work out its relationship with the Free Church Federal Council and with permanent agencies and other ecumenical organisations.

Individual churches will need to consider to what extent their present ways of programming need to be modified in order to fulfil the Swanwick vision of churches working together.

8 Organisational Comments

I Establishment of Churches Together in England

It is proposed that the Commissioning Committee establish an interim Enabling Group to begin work on September 1, 1990 and churches and intermediate bodies will meet as appropriate to appoint their representatives. This interim group will then elect/appoint other officers until the first meeting of the Forum.

II Communication

It is absolutely essential that members of the Forum are kept in contact with the work of Churches Together in England. However this is but a small part of the importance of communication in the life of CTE. A magazine like "Vision One" is needed. This will be useful in communicating information about CTE.

9 Secretariat

Churches Together in England will be staffed initially as follows. These appointments will normally be for five years.

Churches Together in England will be an equal opportunities employer committed to good employment practice. The Enabling Group will keep staffing matters under review, and be responsible for care of staff.

A Staff

1 General Secretary (BCC Grade 1)

Location In an office in the London area.

Task to facilitate and enable the ecumenical bodies in England to fulfil their aims and functions by

(a) Liaison with the headquarters of the member churches
the instrument for Britain and Ireland
the Irish, Scottish and Welsh ecumenical instruments,
the WCC, CEC, and other national bodies internationally
as appropriate.

(b) Servicing the Forum
         the Enabling Group
     To be responsible for supervision of staff.
     To be responsible for general administration.

II Field Officer (North)   (BCC Grade 2)
Location – Sheffield (say)
Task

(a) Liaison with intermediate bodies in the North East, North West, Yorkshire and Humberside, East Midlands, West Midlands.
(b) Liaison with Christian Aid Regional Co-ordinators and with staff of other "agencies" in the North and the Midlands (hereafter, 'the Area'). ("Agencies" include youth officers, social responsibility officers, Association of Inter-Church Families, etc.)
(c) Servicing residential conferences for LEPs and local councils of churches in the Area.
(d) Servicing day meetings for ecumenical officers and officers of intermediate bodies in the Area.
(e) Promotion of CTE matters in the Area and vice versa.
(f) Arranging training courses for ecumenical officers and others with similar remits.
(g) Arranging for induction courses for people in LEPs in the Area.
(h) Member of Forum and of Enabling Group and of LEDAG.
(i) Assist the General Secretary.
(j) Service Northern Church Leaders' Consultation and any other similar gatherings of church leaders.
(k) Service LEDAG jointly with Field Officer (South).

Back-up
Full-time Secretary (BCC Grade 6) with audio and word processing skills
Fully equipped office (preferably not at home)
Adequate finance
A support group drawn from the Area

III Field Officer (South)   (BCC Grade 2)
Location – Didcot (say)
Task

(a) Liaison with intermediate bodies in South West, South East, East Anglia.
(b) to (i) as FO (N) but, of course, in the South.

(j) Attempt to enable and service Southern Church Leaders' gatherings similar to the annual Northern Church Leaders' Consultation.

(k) Service CCLEPE jointly with Field Officer (North).

Back-up as for FO (N)

IV Information and Publications Officer/Office Manager
(BCC Grade 2)

Location – London

Responsible for

      promoting CTE matters in the media

      overseeing publications

      day-to-day administration

      personnel management

      with appropriate support from an advisory group

V Full-time Secretary/PA (BCC Grade 6) in London office with audio and word processing skills.
Responsible for

reception, typing, mail, filing, diary, etc.

VI Full-time Secretary/Accounts Clerk (BCC Grade 6) in London office.
Responsible for

accounts under the guidance of the Hon. Treasurer

assisting the full-time Secretary as needed.

B Possible Costs

At 1990 rates the total cost of salary, pension and National Insurance is as follows:-

General Secretary	£ 20000
FO (N)	£ 18850
FO (S)	£ 18850
Information Officer/Office Manager	£ 18850

A full-time Secretary (BCC Grade 6) would cost in total £12350, so four full-time secretaries — £ 49400

Provision must also be made for the following:-

Travel allowance of approx. £2,200 each for GS, FO (N), FO (S) — £ 6600

Contingencies		
Committee expenses		
Printing and stationery	}	£ 20250
Postage		
Telephone (BCC currently £200.00 per head per annum) 6 x £200.00		£ 1200
Occupancy costs (BCC currently £2000 p.h./p.a.)		£ 12000
	Total	£166000

C   Staff Housing

Churches Together in England will be responsible for housing those staff members who have been dependent on church provision. Where a staff member is housed in CTE accommodation an appropriate deduction will be made from salary towards this. In 1988 this deduction was £3600 per annum.

10 Location of Office

Considerable representation was received from the English regions requesting that the office be sited outside London. The present proposals to have two field officers based outside London will prevent CTE becoming London dominated.

Many of the church responses stated that the office should be located in Inter-Church House with the COCBI office. Their argument was that this was a wise use of space and cheaper than anywhere else. By contrast, the overwhelming view on location of the office expressed by those from the regions and the other nations in Britain and Ireland was that the office should not be in Inter-Church House because it is essential that CTE has, and is seen to have, a separate identity of its own. The Working Party on Churches Together in England agreed with this latter view. However, the Inter-Church Meeting decided that, initially at least, CTE should be located at Inter-Church House.

11 Review and Development

The proposed structures are not intended to be fixed and unchanging. CTE will reflect the developing life of the Christian churches as they continue their pilgrimage together. To take account of progress in the early years it is proposed that not later than September 1, 1993 there shall be set up a review group charged with the task of reporting within one year on the progress of the pilgrimage to date, with proposals for any desirable changes.

The question of Presidency has been discussed but no decision made. It is hoped that CTE will address this early in its existence, together with the question of the relation between CTE and those who customarily speak for the churches.

11 SCOTLAND

The Scottish Steering Committee presented indicative proposals to the churches in January 1988, alongside similar proposals form Working Groups for England, Wales, and Britain and Ireland as a whole. Detailed responses have now been received from the churches, from a variety of organisations, and from a large number of local groups throughout the nation. On the basis of these responses, and operating from the principles outlined above, the Scottish Steering Committee now presents to the Scottish churches the following definitive proposals.

1 Name

The name will be "Action of Churches Together in Scotland" to be known as ACTS.

2 General Purpose

The general purpose of "Action of Churches Together in Scotland", continues the general purpose of Scottish Churches Council, namely "to further the mission and realise the unity of the Church universal by providing a national focus of Inter-Church counsel and action".

3 Basis and Commitment

Action of Churches Together in Scotland (ACTS) (formerly known as Scottish Churches Council) unites in pilgrimage those churches in Scotland which, acknowledging God's revelation in Christ, confess the Lord Jesus Christ as God and Saviour according to the Scriptures and in obedience to God's will and in the power of the Holy Spirit, commit themselves

to seek a deepening of their communion with Christ and with one another in the Church, which is His Body, and

to fulfil their mission to proclaim the Gospel by common witness and service in the world,

to the Glory of the One God, Father, Son and Holy Spirit.

4 Aims

In fulfillment of the general purpose, the churches seek through ACTS:-

4.1 Oneness

to become a fuller realisation of the unity that Christ wills, in accordance with the prayer, "that they all may be one; even as thou, Father art in me, and I in thee, that they also may be in us, that the world may believe that thou has sent me" (John 17.21);

to express the degree of unity that is already theirs by Christ's gift; their commitment to one another, and their resolve to continue as Pilgrims Together;

4.2 Growth of Understanding and Common Life

to grow into a greater unity of mind and heart through experience of each other's living tradition of spirituality and worship;

to co-operate through prayer, theological reflection and consultation, at local and national levels, in all that concerns their common life, especially the nature, purpose and unity of the Church;

to work through joint study towards a Christian evaluation on moral and social issues;

4.3 Unified Action

to co-operate as far as possible in

proclaiming the gospel so as to evoke a personal commitment to Christ and his Church;

obeying the Gospel in practical response to the life and needs of the community, the nation and the world;

witnessing to Christian moral and social values, in a critical phase of human history;

bringing Christian perspectives on the above matters into dialogue with the secular authorities.

5 Membership

ACTS hopes for the widest possible active participation of the Christian community of Scotland.

5.1 Full membership is open to churches which are committed to the Basis and Aims of ACTS.

5.2 Any church which on principle has no credal statements in its tradition and therefore cannot formally subscribe to the statement of faith in the Basis, may nevertheless apply for and be elected to full membership provided it satisfies the member churches which subscribe to the Basis, that it manifest faith in Christ as grounded in the Holy Scriptures, that it is committed to the aims and purposes of ACTS and that it will work in the spirit of the Basis.

5.3 Participant membership is open;

a. to churches which, though eligible, do not wish at this stage to enter into full membership, and

b. to Christian Bodies and Organisations, which confirm their commitment to the Basis and Aims.

5.4 If however any church, Christian tradition or other Christian body were not in sympathy with the Aims or the Basis of ACTS these forms of membership would not be appropriate although observer status may be mutually acceptable.

Explanatory Notes

1 ACTS is a dynamic and developing movement. As such it warmly welcomes the fullest possible participation of all churches and Christian groupings, in the appropriate categories of membership.

2 Full membership is for churches, by which is meant associations of one specific Christian tradition (including bodies organised on the congregational principle). The term "church" therefore would not include such non-denominational and inter-denominational bodies as Student Christian Movement, Scripture Union, National Bible Society, YMCA etc. What is envisaged is a meeting of churches or specific Christian traditions in order to emphasise the place of these bodies in the work of Christian unity.

3 Other Christian bodies have a valued place and a distinctive role as participant members. Their involvement is primarily seen through the functional and working commissions and committees, in which they can play a full and influential part.

6 Structures

6.1 The structures of ACTS maintain the authority of the churches, and enable as many members of the churches as possible to engage in common activity to further the Aims. A feature of the Inter-Church Process has been the participation of so many groups throughout the country. We hope they will continue to form a bridgehead for the activities of ACTS and especially for the major gatherings proposed below. Local co-operation will continue to be central to all the work of ACTS. We encourage all the churches, in making appointments at all levels of ACTS, to hold wherever possible to the Ecumenical Guidelines for Resource Sharing, particularly regarding the participation and representation of women, young people, and lay people.

NOTE:
The Ecumenical Guidelines referred to, developed by the World Consultation on Resource Sharing at EL ESCORIAL recommend, among other things, that there should be "at least 50% women, 50% lay people and 20% young people" in the appointment of representatives.

6.2 Local

Many ecumenical initiatives at local level have happily taken root in various parts of Scotland. These include sharing in prayer and worship, in study and learning, and in witness and service. They represent a growth in fellowship and in warmth of relationships. Much however remains to be done to encourage such activity throughout the land. The challenge to ACTS is to support and make known these initiatives, without seeking in any way to take them over or control them; the need is for promotion, communication, resource-sharing and co-ordination.

In addition to the growth of local inter-church groups, and the continuing work of local councils of churches and clergy fraternals, an increasing number of congregations are entering into some form of association with one or more neighbouring congregations. Such associations are commonly known as 'Local Ecumenical Projects' or 'Ecumenical Parishes'. They vary greatly in form and scope, depending on local needs, opportunities and preferences. All involve some sharing of activities or projects; many include the sharing of resources, of people or facilities; and this sometimes extends to sharing of buildings, or to a measure of team ministry. Where possible, this close association of congregations is expressed in a 'covenant', as a sign of the seriousness of the mutual commitment which is involved.

Focal points in the year, for local ecumenical activity, include the Week of Prayer for Christian Unity, the World Day of Prayer, Holy Week, Christian Aid Week, and One World Week.

6.3 Regional

At Regional level it is proposed that

6.3.1 the churches in their Regional or District manifestations be encouraged to arrange Regional/District Meetings of senior church representatives at least once a year, to relate to public bodies and to encourage local ecumenical development within their Region/District.

6.3.2 the churches of a Region/District be encouraged to appoint, presumably on an honorary or part-time basis, Regional Ecumenical Field Workers, to be agents of stimulation and communication.

6.3.3 Financing to be from the churches or other sources in the Region/District.

6.3.4 The role of churches at national level would be to encourage and facilitate all such local and regional initiatives, learning from them, offering advice and support to them, and enabling them to communicate their experience to others.

6.4 National

At National level the Scottish churches commit themselves progressively to plan and act together in every appropriate area of their life and witness. They therefore understand the proposed structures not as complete expressions of their commitment to one another but as a means of deepening their commitment.

In particular National instruments must as a priority offer resources and service to the development of local and regional ecumenical activity. At National level the following instruments are proposed:

1 Central Council
2 Commissions and Committees
3 Scottish Churches House
4 Scottish Christian Gathering.

The above represent the servicing structures of ACTS. They are financed from the churches' direct contributions, and have a servicing and enabling role in relation to all the other work of the churches together, in the following categories. What follows, refers to the vital common work of the churches together, planned, executed and financed by the churches in a whole variety of ways:

5 Church Agencies and Working Groups
6 Consultations, Networks etc.
7 Scottish Forum

6.5 Central Council

The Central Council will be responsible for discernment of priorities and over-all guidance of common action, which may be initiated through the

Central Council itself, the Commissions or Committees, the Scottish Christian Gathering or the member churches. It will be composed of the holders of leading positions in the churches which are full members together with persons who are in other ways representative of their churches, all appointed by and accountable to these churches. Convenors of the Commissions and Committees named below will also be members of the Central Council in order to ensure its proper links with the working groupings. The Central Council will meet perhaps four times yearly, and will be financed by the general collective budget and staffed by the secretariat. It may appoint sub-groups as required for normal managerial functions e.g. legal trusteeship, finance, publicity, planning etc. Inaugural membership suggested is: Church of Scotland 12, Roman Catholic Church 8, other Member churches 2 each together with the Convenors of Commissions and Committees (totalling 8 at present).

6.6 Commissions and Committees

6.6.1 We propose, as part of the servicing structure related to the Central Council, three Commissions and five Committees. Commissions operate in broad functional or thematic areas of concern; Committees relate a particular constituency or concern to ACTS as a whole.

6.6.2 Commissions – we propose the establishment of three Commissions responsible to the churches for shared thinking and for guidance on major areas of common concern. The Commissions would also relate to, encourage, and co-ordinate the work of existing or new agencies of the churches in the broad area concerned. They are:

Commission on Christian Unity
Commission on Mission, Evangelism and Education
Commission on Justice and Peace; Social and Moral Issues

6.6.3 Committees have a different character in that they seek to relate all these functional areas above to a particular constituency or need. We see 5 Committees as necessary at the inaugural stage.

Committee on Local and Regional Unity
Committee on Communications
Committee on Youth participation
Committee on Women's participation
Committee on Scottish Churches House

6.6.4 These committees, like all parts of the servicing structures, exist to enable but not to control. They recognise the many creative things which are already happening, often in ecumenical ways, in these areas, but seek to ensure that these broad concerns are represented in the central servicing structures.

6.6.5 All Commissions and Committees will consist of representatives appointed directly by the churches, in numbers and proportions to be decided by the Central Council. Normally they would include those with direct responsibility in the churches for the particular area of concern. Commissions and Committees will also include representation from the Christian Groups, Organisations and Agencies active in the particular area. Commissions and Committees will report both to the Central Council and directly to the member churches.

6.6.6 The foregoing structure of Commissions and Committees may appear rather complex; but in fact bodies are already in existence covering all the above interests and concerns.

6.7 Appointments

In all servicing structures of ACTS, churches will seek to make their appointments as representative as possible, and to observe a degree of proportionality among the churches. The Central Council and the Commissions will not normally discern the mind of the meeting by voting, but by reaching a broad consensus through prayer and deliberation.

6.8 Scottish Churches House Dunblane

6.8.1 Scottish Churches House was established more than 25 years ago as a Conference Centre and Meeting Place for all the churches in Scotland. For most of that time it has also been the main office of Scottish Churches Council, to whom the house belongs. It is in constant use by all kinds of church groups and many secular bodies. It is also used by the Council's Committees and for consultations on topics of importance for the church or the nation. The contribution of the house to the unity and mission of the Scottish churches cannot be over-estimated and it is a much loved place of meeting and retreat. The House will certainly support and underpin many of these activities and frequently act as the meeting place for ACTS.

6.8.2 There should be a Director of Scottish Churches House, who is not the General Secretary, but who might combine this post with responsibility for another of the major areas defined in the Commissions and Committees above.

6.9 Scottish Christian Gathering

A Scottish Christian Gathering is proposed for celebration and vision, fellowship, exploration and discernment of opportunities and tasks; with broad participation from all member churches and others, to amplify and strengthen the whole movement of ACTS. The Gathering would receive input from all the commissions, committees, agencies etc and give impetus to them. It would also provide an opportunity for members of "Pilgrim Groups" all over the country to come together and express their mind in Christ. Membership would be large, possibly of the order of 1,000, drawn from throughout the nation and including all members of Central Council, Other Bodies and Commissions. The Gathering would be convened at intervals, possibly every second year; financing would be dependent on size, but self-financing would be preferred, with some possible subsidy from the churches for their members participating.

6.10 Secretariat and Staff

To service the new instruments effectively requires 4 senior staff members and appropriate secretarial and other support staff. There should be a General Secretary whose role is to co-ordinate, enable and provide imaginative leadership to the whole operation and ensure its linkage with the Central Council and with the churches. An effective Administrative Secretary is also needed. The four senior staff members forming the secretariat would therefore be: a General Secretary, an Adminstrative Secretary, and two associates, who together would share responsibilities for the areas covered by the three Commissions, and for Scottish Churches House; the areas covered by the other Committees above would either also be shared among the full-time secretariat, or serviced in other ways as agreed by the churches.

6.11 Church Agencies, Working Groups, Consultations, Networks etc.

6.11.1 Church Agencies and Working Groups are organisations which exist on a permanent basis for a particular piece of common work. They include at present such bodies as;

Christian Aid
Scottish Catholic International Aid Fund
Scottish Agency for Adult Christian Education
Christian Enquiry Agency
Scottish Churches Action for World Development
Scottish Churches Group for Justice, Peace and the Integrity of Creation
Scottish Churches Community and Race Relations Group
Scottish Churches Youth Service

These Agencies are organised and financed by the churches in a variety of different ways, and offer several models of how such work might be continued, developed and further integrated.

6.11.2 Networks and Consultations are less permanent groupings which come together for particular purposes on a shorter term or occasional basis.

6.11.3 All the above agencies, networks etc could be serviced by the appropriate staff of the churches working together, by one church acting on behalf of all, by specially appointed staff, or in a variety of other agreed ways. They would normally be financed and sustained by the churches' own budgets and resources, operating within agreed strategies.

6.12 Scottish Forum

We welcome the presence of church representatives, with those of a wide variety of Scottish institutions and groupings, in a number of actual and proposed bodies which are seeking to articulate Scottish opinion and present a coherent Scottish voice. In addition, it will remain open to ACTS from time to time to set up a Forum for the discussion of national questions. We hope that Scottish Churches House could maintain and develop its central position as a "Third Place" where people of all views and organisations can meet to clarify and understand issues.

7 Finances

7.1 The member churches will make regular annual financial contributions to a collective budget, to cover the cost of the Central Council, Commissions, Gatherings and Staff of ACTS. This is comparable to the system for financing the present Scottish Churches Council.

7.2 ACTS will co-operate with the Council of Churches for Britain and Ireland in agreeing and presenting a combined asking, for all churches which are members of both instruments. This will be done every three years to cover the following three year period.

7.3 For churches at present in membership of the Scottish Churches Council and the British Council of Churches the combined asking for the first year of the life of the new instruments will not exceed the sum of the askings of them in the last year of the life of the Scottish Churches Council and the British Council of Churches, allowing only for inflation.

7.4 It is anticipated that in both instruments the increase in the number of member churches will increase the scope of their work, though the new 'enabling' style means their work may sometimes depend more directly on the churches. Any consequent increase in the total expenditure of the new instruments combined will be offset by additional income from the new members.

7.5 It is anticipated that the change in the style, agenda and structure of the new instruments will entail a limited shift towards the Scottish Instrument in the balance of contributions, further increasing income (see note below).

7.6 In the first instance, the relative levels of contribution asked of the member churches will be broadly related to the relative sizes of their membership, the contribution of the Roman Catholic Church and the Church of Scotland, for example, relating to one another approximately in the ratio of 2:3.

7.7 After ACTS comes into being, a more precise measure for determining contributions may be devised; it may be based on churches' membership, income, size of representation on the body, or other factors.

7.8 Churches and Bodies in participant membership will be asked for appropriate contributions, to be determined by ACTS after it is established.

7.9 If two or more churches judge that new work requires to be undertaken in any field and also judge it would be wise to undertake this new work together, they will finance it from their own budgets, as they would if the new work were undertaken separately. Such work undertaken together will not entail greater expenditure and may require less expenditure than if it were undertaken separately.

7.10 Similarly, if two or more churches agree to undertake together any work which at present they undertake separately, there will be no additional expenditure and there may be a saving.

7.11 Thus the new quality of commitment asked of the churches through the Inter-Church Process will be expressed not in any increase in their contributions to the combined budget of the new bodies, but in their progressive willingness to use their resources together or in a common strategy, in all appropriate areas of their common life and witness.

NOTE:
The preliminary estimated budget for ACTS in its first year is c. £130,000. This compares with the budget of Scottish Churches Council in its last year of c. £100,000.

There must be an intensive process of consultation based on common criteria, to ensure that detailed and complementary budgets for all the new instruments are produced as soon as possible.

8 Ensuring Complementary Structures

It is essential that there should be a far greater degree of integration, than has been the case with the previous ecumenical bodies. This should be assured in a number of ways:

8.1 The staff of ACTS should be in regular contact with the equivalent co-ordinating staff of the British and Irish Body.

8.2 At the level of the Central Council in Scotland, and the Assembly and Church Representatives Meeting in Britain and Ireland, we believe the churches must ensure that there is an adequate overlap of membership. We recognise the difficulties here but think it essential for proper complementary working. In both cases the churches appoint their representatives directly.

8.3 In the case of the functional and working structures. i.e. the Commissions and Committees in Scotland, and their British equivalent Bodies, the same arrangement as above might apply. As an alternative however the Scottish churches might consider joint representation on some working Commissions of the British Instrument, i.e. that the appropriate Scottish Commission or Committee could nominate an agreed number of representatives from their own group to attend the parallel meeting at the British level. This could help integration, save considerable resources, help the smaller churches to feel better represented, and could also represent the reality of a situation where the Scottish churches are often able to speak with a common voice on many issues.

9 Conclusion

We believe that the above proposals are true to the vision of the Inter-Church Process, are flexible and provisional, and can be an effective means by which the Scottish churches may give substance to their commitment to one another, and their common commitment to the one God, Father, Son and Holy Spirit.

12 WALES

Our proposal is that the Council of Churches for Wales (CCW) shall be succeeded by a new body with the following characteristics:

1 Name

1.1 For the new body we propose the short name

CYTUN

followed, whenever appropriate, by the fuller title

CHURCHES TOGETHER IN WALES

1.2 CYTUN (pronounced CĂTĒĒN), means 'Together'. It is the word used, for example, in the 1588 Welsh Bible of the church at Pentecost in Acts 2 1, and in the 1988 New Welsh Bible of the call to Christian unity in Romans 15 5. It is an acronym of Cristnogion ymiaen tuag at undeb (Christians forward towards unity).

2 Basis and Commitment

The following is being proposed, subject to counsel's opinion:

CYTUN: Churches Together in Wales (formerly known as the Council of Churches for Wales) unites in pilgrimage those churches in Wales which, acknowledging God's revelation in Christ, confess the Lord Jesus Christ as God and Saviour according to the Scriptures; and, in obedience to God's will and in the power of the Holy Spirit, commit themselves

to seek a deepening of their communion with Christ and with one another in the Church, which is his body, and

to fulfil their mission to proclaim the Gospel by common witness and service in the world,

to the glory of the one God, Father, Son and Holy Spirit.

3 Aims and Functions

3.1 Those who were present at the Bangor and Swanwick conferences of the *Not Strangers but Pilgrims* process bear testimony to having received a new experience of the power of God to create unity out of a hitherto unparalleled diversity of Christian traditions.

3.2 CYTUN will gather together the churches of Wales in all the richness of their present diversity

> of denomination and tradition;
> of race and language,
> of men and women, young and old,
> of lay and ordained,

so that they can learn from and value each others' traditions in a parity of esteem wherein none is felt disregard or devalued.

3.3 It will seek to enable the churches to do together whatever they can, either pooling their resources or allowing one church or agency to act on behalf of others; and to do all other things in the light of the insights and understandings of others.

3.4 It will act as a body which enables the churches themselves to reach their decisions in the context of common study, prayer and worship. It will not be a "super church" and will seek to avoid becoming an ecclesiastical bureaucracy.

3.5 It will seek to help the churches to arrive at a common mind so that they might become more fully united in faith, communion, pastoral care and mission.

3.6 It will seek to become, through the power of the Holy Spirit, such a sign of that growing unity as will authenticate the churches' common call

> to individual repentance,
> to the renewal of our corporate life, and
> to the proclamation of the gospel of God's reconciliation

in a divided nation and a divided world.

3.7 It will offer the churches the opportunity to a enter into a new commitment

> to reflect together theologically on matters of faith, order and ethics;
> to pray together and to learn to appreciate each other's patterns of prayer;
> to work together, sharing resources and presenting the Gospel in word and action.

4 Membership

4.1 The following categories of Membership listed in section 5 (p. 17 above) will be available to churches and other bodies within Wales, and with the conditions specified therein, namely, Full Membership (paras. 1-2); Bodies in Association (para. 3). We do not anticipate the need in Wales for the proposed category of Associate Membership (para. 4).

4.2 Churches and associations of churches in full membership will be entitled to places on Y Gymanfa, the Council and Steering Committee (see below, 5.1.2., 5.2.2., 5.3.2.); Bodies in Association (which we anticipate will include the Free Church Council, Sunday School Council, YW/YMCA, SCM, NACCAN etc.) will be entitled to places on Y Gymanfa (see below, 5.1.2.2.) and will be encouraged to play a full part in the life of the Commissions, Networks and Working Parties.

4.3 **Observers.** In addition the category of Observer status will be available to those churches and associations of churches which either do not fully meet the requirements for Full Membership or do not wish to take up the full duties and privileges of Full Membership. Observer churches will be entitled to be represented on Y Gymanfa and the Council on the same basis as full members, to speak at meetings, but not to vote. Observer churches will be encouraged to make appropriate contributions to the work of CYTUN.

5 Structures

CYTUN will operate through following bodies:

5.1 Y Gymanfa (The Assembly)

5.1.1 Y Gymanfa (which we recommend should normally be known by its Welsh name) will

5.1.1.1 provide an opportunity for Christians in Wales to celebrate their unity in Christ;

5.1.1.2 conduct most of its business in a participatory style of working;

5.1.1.3 derive its agenda from concerns raised by
local Councils of Churches, local Covenants, Local Ecumenical Projects; members churches of CYTUN;
the constituent parts of CYTUN;
the Council of Churches for Britain and Ireland and world ecumenical bodies.

5.1.1.4 set the general direction of CYTUN's work during the following period;

5.1.1.5 normally channel its concerns on public issues to the churches via the appropriate element of CYTUN.

5.1.2 Y Gymanfa will be composed of approximately 150 members, of whom

5.1.2.1 two thirds will be appointed by the churches in full membership. Each church, however small, will have a basic representation of four; the remaining places in this category will be divided between the larger churches in proportion to the number of their members, as notified by each church to the secretariat.

Notes:
1 In Appendix 1 we have given a calculation of this distribution on the basis of figures currently available to the Working Party.
2 The persons appointed by each member church to the Council will normally be among its representatives to Y Gymanfa.

5.1.2.2 one third will be representative of local Councils of Churches, officers of CYTUN, bodies in association and observer churches. These places will be allocated on a basis to be determined from time to time by the Steering Committee.

5.1.3 Y Gymanfa should meet every two or three years, for a period of 48 hours, at a time when it is possible for the greatest variety of people to be present. It will meet either residentially at a Conference Centre/University Campus or non-residentially with hospitality provided by the local Christian community.

5.2 **The Council**

5.2.1 The Council will

5.2.1.1 collate the concerns of the churches nationally and of those working ecumenically locally and in the regions,

5.2.1.2 be responsible for co-ordinating the work of Y Gymanfa, of the Commissions, Networks and Working Parties, and for CYTUN's resources and staffing.

5.2.1.3 monitor the progress made in the churches and in CYTUN towards the implementation of proposals for
Sharing of Resources Ecumenically (See, for example, the WCC Guidelines from El Escorial);
Participation and Representation (See above p. 19);

5.2.1.4 will elect, from a different tradition in rotation, one President and two Vice-presidents to serve for two years, who will as appropriate chair meetings of Y Gymanfa and the Council. It will also appoint from time to time Moderators for the Commissions and for the Steering Committee.

5.2.2 The Council will be composed of approximately 50 members, who will include leaders of the member churches nationally.

5.2.2.1 Each church, however small, will have a basic membership of two; the remaining places will be divided between the larger churches in proportion to the number of their members, as notified by each church to the secretariat.

Notes:

1 In Appendix 1 we have given a calculation of this distribution on the bases of figures currently available to the Working Party.

2 As far as possible churches will endeavour to make their members representative of their regional structure, of the laity and the clergy, of women and men, and of young people. They will move towards appointing representatives for periods of three years.

5.2.2.2 Officers of CYTUN and Moderators of the Commissions will be invited to attend as non-voting members.

5.2.3 The Council will normally meet twice a year.

5.3 The Steering Committee

5.3.1 The Steering Committee will

5.3.1.1 be responsible for the implementation of policies laid down by Y Gymanfa and by the Council;

5.3.1.2 recommend how particular pieces of work should be undertaken, whether within the various parts of CYTUN, or by one church on behalf of the churches.

5.3.2 The Steering Committee will be composed of one person from each church in full membership, normally its principal administrative or ecumenical officer. A limited number of officers of CYTUN and the Commissions will be invited to attend as non-voting members. It will normally meet at least four times a year.

5.4 Commissions

A principal means by which the churches will work out ther commitment to one another will be by setting up Commissions (which in our Interim Report (para. 34.2) we called Agencies).

5.4.1 Commissions will be designed to enable the churches to engage together in responsible shared thinking, to offer guidance to them on major issues of common concern, and, where appropriate, to enable them to engage in common action. They will report from time to time to the Council, but will be responsible directly to the member churches.

5.4.2 They will normally be composed of two members from each church in full membership. They will have power to co-opt individuals with particular expertise and representatives of relevant associated bodies and observer churches.

5.4.3 They will advise the churches how best particular pieces of work within their remit should be undertaken, whether by one church on behalf of all, or with the participation of others, or by an ecumenical programme.

5.4.4 They will seek to appropriate within Wales work done within their remit by the Agencies and Commissions and Networks of the Council of Churches for Britain and Ireland, the Conference of European Churches and the World Council of Churches.

5.4.5 Their main administrative costs will be a charge on the budget of CYTUN. Major items of new expenditure will be subject to the approval of the Council.

5.4.6 Initially we envisage the setting up of three Commissions:

5.4.6.1 **The Commission for Ecumenical Affairs** will

— foster shared thinking on matters of faith and order;

— foster a common spirituality in relation to the whole life and mission of the churches in Wales and world-wide;

— seek to widen and deepen the work of local Free Church Councils and Councils of Churches, promote appropriate patterns of regional ecumenism and offer guidance to the churches on their participation in Local Ecumenical Projects, Local Covenants etc., and

— explore the relationship between the Covenant for Union in Wales and the wider search for Christian unity.

5.4.6.2 **The Commission for Evangelism** will take further the work presently being undertaken within the Department of World Mission and by Wales for Christ. It will

— reflect upon how the Gospel has to be presented within the ever-changing social, political, environmental, and intellectual context in Wales:

— explore, and strive to extend, the limits of co-operation in presenting the gospel among the member churches;

— evaluate and develop methods and strategies for evangelism;

— disseminate insights gained through our participation in the proposed British and Irish Commission on Mission, and through our links with the World Church;

– explore and develop appropriate links with people of other faith communities, and

– stimulate local activity, by providing information and training for those engaged in Christian witness.

5.4.6.3 **The Commission for National Affairs** will be the means by which the churches in Wales commit themselves to doing their social responsibility work in an ecumenical manner. It will not be narrowly concerned with Welsh affairs, but will also be the means of bringing perspectives arising in Wales to bear upon the British, European and world scenes, and allowing insights gained from our involvements outside Wales to bear upon Welsh life. For example, it will

– give the churches an opportunity to understand better each others' perspectives on ethical issues;

– enable the churches to reach a common mind and take common action within Wales on social, educational, economic, industrial and environmental questions;

– further the churches' concern in Wales for justice, peace and the integrity of creation, and

– seek to develop appropriate links on behalf of the churches with the Welsh Office, Welsh MPs, MEPs, industry, trades unions etc.

5.4.7 We anticipate that in the course of time the work of the Networks, described below, will lead to the creation of further Commissions.

5.5 **Networks**

5.5.1 Networks are called for in all those areas of church life which are not covered by one or other of the above Commissions. They will link together those persons within the churches who have responsibility for a particular area of work together with representatives of relevant associated bodies.

5.5.2 Their functions will be:

- to co-ordinate work being undertaken by the member churches;

- to enable other member churches to own work done by one church;

- to prepare the way for the creation of further Commissions;

- to help the churches appropriate work being done within their field by the Council of Churches for Britain and Ireland.

5.5.3 Examples of areas where Networks will be appropriate are:

Community workers.
Theological educators.
Those engaged in public education.

Youth officers.

Children's Work Officers, together with Sunday School Council officers.

Stewardship/Care of church buildings officers.

Editors of church papers, publications managers.

Press officers and those engaged in local and national broadcasting.

5.6 Working Parties

5.6.1 Working Parties are groups set up for a limited duration in order to undertake a particular piece of work.(In our Interim Report para. 34.3 we called them Task Forces.)

5.6.2 Some will be set up by the Council in order to explore newly arising concerns; their costs would be a charge on the budget of CYTUN.

5.6.3 Others will be set up by one of the Commissions and will be a charge on its budget. Others again may be set up by Networks, or by one or more churches which choose to take a lead in a matter; these might then be owned by others. Such Working Parties would only be a charge on the budget of CYTUN with the approval of the Council.

5.6.4 Any piece of work currently being undertaken by CCW on 31.8.90 which is not catered for otherwise, should be regarded as a Working Party, responsible to the Council.

6 Maintaining Present Relationships

6.1 While it is clear that CYTUN will be a new body which must be free to develop its work in its own way, it will inherit from the Council of Churches for Wales a body of close and fruitful relationships which have developed over the years. In this section we shall seek to give a number of examples of ways in which we anticipate the transition from the old to the new will take place. We would emphasise that what follows is provisional only and is open to further discussion between the parties concerned.

6.2 With the Commission of the Covenanted Churches

6.2.1 In the Interim Report (para. 36.1.) we indicated that the nature of this relationship in the future would depend to a considerable extent upon the responses the Covenanted Churches would make to *Ministry in a Uniting Church*. Those responses are now known. Whereas some of the Covenanted Churches have encouraged the Commission to proceed within the terms outlined in the report, others have asked for further clarification on certain fundamental questions before they could recommend such steps to be taken. Although the Commission had hoped for a more positive response to its proposals it has nevertheless found much encouragement in the churches' decisions.

6.2.2 Of central importance is the conviction that the Covenanted Churches remain committed to the Covenant as an effective way towards visible unity. The Commission will therefore continue to pursue its goal of enabling the Covenanted Churches, on the basis of the recognition acknowledged in the first clause of each article of the Covenant, to work out in their shared life and mission, the intentions to which they pledged themselves in the second clauses and thus to reach deeper agreement on faith, mission, the nature of the church, membership, ministry, worship and the government of the church. In order that all the churches may better understand the nature of this commitment of the Covenanted Churches to one another, and to judge how it relates to the commitment they are invited to make in response to the *Not Strangers but Pilgrims* Inter-Church Process, we are setting out the text of the Covenant in Appendix II.

6.2.3 As a contribution to this ongoing search for visible unity the Commission will prepare a response to the clarification on ministry requested by the churches and will receive during 1989 the first report of its Baptism, Initiation and Membership Group.

6.2.4 The churches gave particular encouragement to the Commission to develop patterns of local initiatives through Local Acts of Reconciliation, Local Covenants and Ecumenical Projects. Around 60 such projects already exist throughout Wales, many involving Covenanted Churches. The Commission intends to give priority to enabling further developments of this kind and has set up a Working Party to plan and co-ordinate its work in this field.

5.2.5 These priorities represent what the Commission sees as 'the sharp edge of the Covenant'. It is therefore being proposed to the Covenanted Churches that the Commission should continue in its present form with these priorities, that it should appoint on a half-time basis its own General Secretary, Field Officer, and that its administration and funding should be separate from those of CYTUN. Consequently the Commission is proposing to the Covenanted Churches, simultaneously with the publication of this report, a pattern of administration, staffing and funding for the period September 1st 1990 onwards.

6.2.6 At the same time it believes that a close relationship between the Commission of Covenanted Churches and CYTUN would be vitally important. This relationship would be primarily through the Commission for Ecumenical Affairs, which has as one its aims to explore the inner-relationship, locally and nationally, between the search for visible unity by the Covenanted Churches and the Commitment of all the Churches within the Inter-Church Process to be 'pilgrims together'.

6.3 With Christian Aid

6.3.1 Christian Aid is an important and special case. It has long enjoyed a close and warm relationship with CCW. Christian Aid itself has developed a number of important administrative and eductational functions to its staff in Wales. We are anxious that these arrangements should continue. In the immediate future, however, it will be important to establish equally close relationships with CAFOD, the equivalent Roman Catholic organisation.

6.3.2 In its response to the working parties' initial reports Christian Aid is anxious to ensure to ensure for the future that its priorities (as, for instance, they have ben set down in *To Strengthen the Poor*) should be the priorities of the churches, and that it should be seen not as an autonomous agency, but, as it has always claimed to be, "the churches in action with the world's poor".

6.3.3 In order to achieve these ends it is being proposed that Christian Aid should become directly responsible to the churches (see below p.94). It is desirable that Christian Aid/Cymru should likewise be related closely to the Welsh churches via CYTUN. It would then have a position analogous to the Commissions outlined above. However it is important that a close relationship should develop between Christian Aid and each of the commissions: with the Commission for Ecumenical Affairs through the close working of its regional officers with the Commission's regional network; with the Commission for Evangelism as *To Strengthen the Poor* becomes an integral part of the churches' proclamation; and with the Commission for National Affairs through its work of development education. It is from work together at these levels, we believe, that the desired closer links between CYTUN, Christian Aid and CAFOD/Cymru will emerge.

6.4 With the Free Church Council for Wales

We anticipate that the Free Church Council for Wales will become a Body in Association with CYTUN and that it will principally relate to the Council through the Commission for Ecumenical Affairs, its officers being co-opted members of the Commission.

6.5 Christian Enquiry Agency, if and when it is set up in Wales, might appropriately be regarded as a programme under the auspices of the Commission for Evangelism.

6.6 Christians Against Torture is a campaign which has for some years been sponsored by the Council of Churches for Wales. We anticipate that it will continue in its present form but under the auspices of the Commission for National Affairs.

7 Officers and Secretariat

7.1 Officers

The Officers of CYTUN (see, e.g., 5.2.2.2., 5.3.2.) will be the President, the two Vice-Presidents, the General Secretary and the Honorary Treasurer. For the appointment of the President and Vice-Presidents, see above, 5.2.1.4.

7.2 The General Secretariat

7.2.1 CYTUN will be served by a full-time General Secretary and a full-time Administrative Assistant.

7.2.2 The General Secretary will be responsible for

   – the over-all co-ordination of the Council's work, and in particular for servicing meetings of Y Gymanfa, the Council and the Steering Committee;

   – maintaining links with the other ecumenical bodies in Britain and Ireland;

   – maintaining links with local Councils of Churches, and developing and co-ordinating a network of regional ecumenical officers, seconded by the churches, in conjunction with the Commission for Ecumenical Affairs.

7.2.3 The General Secretariat will continue to be housed in the present premises in St Helen's Road, Swansea.

7.3 The Commissions

7.3.1 Initially the Commissions will look to the churches to second suitably qualified persons to direct their work on a part-time basis. Whether this pattern will be adequate in the longer term is something which the churches will have to decide in the light of experience.

7.3.2 The offices of those directing the work of the Commissions would be housed in premises belonging to the churches seconding officers.

7.4 **Other officers.** Networks and Working Parties will normally be serviced by members appointed from within the groups. The Treasurership will be an honorary appointment, with day-to-day book-keeping undertaken by the Administrative Assistant.

8 Finance

It will be clear from the foregoing that member churches will be contributing to the work of CYTUN in two ways, in cash and in kind.

8.1 Contributions in kind

These take two forms: when churches undertake a particular piece of work on behalf of other churches, and when they second members of staff to work on behalf of CYTUN. Since is it impossible to quantify such contributions accurately, and since they will be made where a particular church's priorities coincide with the needs of CYTUN, they should not be taken into account when assessing churches' cash contributions.

8.2 Cash contributions

8.2.1 The churches' cash contributions will be based on the principles and methods of assessment contained in the paragraphs above on **Financing the New Bodies** (see p.25). There it is proposed that the member churches' contributions for the first three year period will be based on their 1990 figure adjusted annually according to the annual inflation rate (see Note 3 of the above document). However, this is complicated in Wales by the fact that hitherto the Covenanted Churches have contributed at a higher rate than other churches in order to meet the running costs of the Commission of Covenanted Churches. It is further complicated in that it is being proposed that in future the costs of that Commission should be met separately from those of CYTUN.

8.2.2 It is important that CYTUN, in contrast to its predecessor, should be adequately funded. Membership carries with it the responsibility of contributing fully to its work. We believe that as quickly as possible this should be achieved by all the churches paying an equal contribution per church member.

8.2.3 The proposed budget of expenditure for the initial year of the first three year period, amounting to approximately £52,000 (see Appendix III), is based on the pattern of CCW expenditure for 1990 with an addition of 5% for inflation, plus further additions which take into account the proposed programme of CYTUN.

8.2.4 In order to meet the cost of the expenditure proposed in Appendix III soley from within Wales and on the basis of equal contributions, a contribution of 12½p per member would be required (the pattern of contributions which results is illustrated in Appendix IV).

8.2.5 However it is recognised that some churches, particularly those not within the Covenant, will find this an extremely difficult challenge to meet in the short term. Attention is here drawn to the proposal in **Financing the New Bodies** (para b. and Note 6) that both the churches' contributions to the new bodies and the allocation of funding between them will be brought together so that there can be a co-ordinated approach throughout Britain and Ireland. It is recognised that initially CYTUN may need to benefit from this procedure.

8.2.6 In order to alleviate this situation and enable the Welsh churches to pay their own way as quickly as possible, the following transitional arrangements are suggested:

8.2.6.1 For 1990-91 all churches will be asked to contribute a **minimum** of 10p per church member, and those that can are asked to contribute up to 15p per church member (See Appendix IV).

8.2.6.2 It is hoped that those churches contributing 10p per member in 1990-91 will be able to contribute proportionately more in the following years.

8.2.6.3 After the first triennium it is suggested that all churches pay at the same level either on the basis of church membership (currently 12½p per member) or by whatever alternative method is agreed within CYTUN and within the new bodies as a whole.

8.3 At present local Councils of Churches pay a small affiliation fee to CCW. We believe that the links between the local and national levels will be strengthened in CYTUN. As this happens, and as the local councils see that they are getting a better service from the new body, e.g., through field workers, they will want in due course to increase these contributions.

8.4 We believe that the responsibility for funding the work of CYTUN should rest directly upon the churches. We would therefore encourage the Friends of CCW to wind up its operation and hand over any outstanding funds to the existing Council.

Appendix I
Composition of Y Gymanfa and the Council

The following breakdown is given on the basis of currently available figures as an indication of the likely composition of these bodies. For the purpose of these calculations, larger churches are defined as those with more than 5000 members.

Church	Membership in '000s	Y Gymanfa	The Council
BUGB	14	6	3
BUW	35	9	5
C in W	110	20	10
Methodist	25	8	4
PCW	70	14	7

RCC	100	18	9
RS/Friends	0.4	4	2
Sal. Army	2.5	4	2
Undeb Ann.	55	12	6
URC	7	5	3
Totals	418.9	100*	51

*In addition, fifty other members will be appointed by a different process (see 5.1.2.2.).

Appendix II
The Welsh Covenant

The text of the Covenant which the Church in Wales, the Presbyterian Church in Wales, the Methodist Church and the United Reformed Church, together with a number of Baptist Churches, entered in 1975 is as follows. It is set out here for information, and in order that the churches may judge for themselves the nature of the commitment which the Covenanted Churches have already made to one another, and how it compares with that implied in membership of CYTUN (see Aims and Functions, para. 3 above.)

The Covenant

Confessing our faith in Jesus Christ as Lord and Saviour, and renewing our will to serve his mission in the world, our several churches have been brought into a new relationship with one another. Together we give thanks for all we have in common. Together we repent the sin of perpetuating our division. Together we make known our understanding of the obedience to which we are called:

1. (a) We recognize in one another the same faith in the gospel of Jesus Christ found in Holy Scripture, which the creeds of the ancient Church and other historic confessions are intended to safeguard. We recognize in one another the same desire to hold this faith in its fulness.

   (b) We intend so to act, speak, and serve together in obedience to the gospel that we may learn more of its fulness and make it known to others in contemporary terms and by credible witness.

2. (a) We recognize in one another the same awareness of God's calling to serve his gracious purpose for all mankind, with particular responsibility for this land and people.

(b) We intend to work together for justice and peace at home and abroad, and for the spiritual and material well-being and personal freedom of all people.

3 (a) We recognize one another as within the one Church of Jesus Christ, pledged to serve His Kingdom, and sharing in the unity of the Spirit.

(b) We intend by the help of the same Spirit to overcome the divisions which impair our witness, impede God's mission, and obscure the gospel of man's salvation, and to manifest that unity which is in accordance with Christ's will.

4 (a) We recognize the members of all our churches as members of Christ in virtue of their common baptism and common calling to participate in the ministry of the whole Church.

(b) We intend to seek that form of common life which will enable each member to use the gifts bestowed upon him in the service of Christ's Kingdom.

5 (a) We recognize the ordained ministries of all our churches as true ministries of the word and sacraments, through which God's love is proclaimed, his grace mediated, and his Fatherly care exercised.

(b) We intend to seek an agreed pattern of ordained ministry which will serve the gospel in unity, manifest its continuity throughout the ages, and be accepted as far as may be by the Church throughout the world.

6 (a) We recognize in one another patterns of worship and sacramental life, marks of holiness and zeal, which are manifestly gifts of Christ.

(b) We intend to listen to one another and to study together the witness and practice of our various traditions, in order that the riches entrusted to us in separation may be preserved for the united Church which we seek.

7 (a) We recognize in one another the same concern for the good government of the Church for the fulfilment of its mission.

(b) We intend to seek a mode of Church government which will preserve the positive values for which each has stood, so that the common mind of the Church may be formed and carried into action through constitutional organs of corporate decision at every level of responsibility.

We do not yet know the form union will take. We approach our task with openness to the Spirit. We believe that God will guide his Church into ways of truth and peace, correcting, strengthening, and renewing it in accordance with the mind of Christ. We therefore urge all our members to accept one another in the Holy Spirit as Jesus Christ accepts us, and to avail themselves of every opportunity to grow together through common prayer and worship in mutual understanding and love so that in every place they may be renewed together for mission.

Accordingly we enter now into this solemn Covenant before God and with one another, to work and pray in common obedience to our Lord Jesus Christ, in order that by the Holy Spirit we may be brought into one visible Church to serve together in mission to the glory of God the Father.

Appendix III

Proposed Income Budget for CYTUN 1990-91

Salaries and Staff Expenses	29500
Office and Staff Expenses	11000
Committee etc. Administration Costs	9000
Capital Costs	2800
	£52300

Appendix IV

Proposed Income Budget for CYTUN 1990-91

	(at 12½p)	(at 10p)	(at 15p)
Church in Wales	13750	11000	16500
Presbyterian Church of Wales	8750	7000	10500
Union of Welsh Independants	6875	5500	8250
The Methodist Church	3125	2500	3750
The Baptist Union of Wales	4375	3500	5350
The Baptist Union of G.B.	1750	1400	2100
The United Reformed Church	875	700	1050
The Salvation Army	250	200	300
The Religious Society of Friends	50	40	60
The Roman Catholic Church	12500	10000	15000
	£52300	£41840	£62820

13 IRELAND

1   All the major churches in Ireland serve the whole island. Therefore it is inappropriate that a body with which any of these churches is related should simply be called 'British', and in the proposals which follow the title 'Council of Churches for Britain and Ireland' is put forward.

2   Formal inter-church relations in Ireland are conducted through the following structures.

a) The Irish Council of Churches first met in 1923 and has as member churches the Church of Ireland (Anglican), Lutheran, Methodist, Moravian, Non-Subscribing Presbyterian and Presbyterian Churches, the Salvation Army and the Religious Society of Friends. It works by means of its Boards of Inter-Church, Community and Overseas Affairs, and co-operates closely with the Roman Catholic Irish Commission for Justice and Peace in a Peace Education programme. Also, Roman Catholic observers attend meetings of the Council.

b) The Irish Inter-Church Meeting (popularly known as 'Ballymascanlon') brings together the member churches of the Irish Council of Churches and the Roman Catholic Church in Ireland. First meeting in 1973, it was restructured in 1985 with an organising Committee and Departments of Theology and Social Issues. A number of reports have been published, understanding has grown and inter-church bible study has been encouraged. This Inter-Church Meeting gives an opportunity for all Irish churches to co-operate, and exists alongside the Irish Council of Churches from which it remains distinct.

c) The Inter-Church Consultative Committee was set up in 1985 "to help those involved in existing joint schemes" in which there is Church of Ireland and Methodist, or Methodist and Presbyterian co-operation. The Committee has initiated a review of those schemes already in existence for a number of years.

3   The Church of Ireland, Methodist and Presbyterian Churches in Ireland have been members of the BCC from its formation.

4   From the beginning of the Not Strangers But Pilgrims Inter-Church Process the Irish churches which have membership of the BCC have participated with observer status. At the Swanwick Conference the Irish Inter-Church Committee ('Ballymascanlon') was represented by the Revd Gerry Clifford (Roman Catholic) and the Revd David Nesbitt (ICC).

5 As outlined above, the Irish churches have developed their own ways of ecumenical fellowship, e.g. in the 'Ballymascanlon' process, and would place Irish inter-church relationships as their first, but not exclusive, priority.

6 The Roman Catholic Church in Ireland has not so far been a member church of the Not Strangers But Pilgrims Inter-Church Process. Discussion between the churches is taking place, and at the present time no decisions have been taken about the churches' future relationship to the Council of Churches for Britain and Ireland. The door is wide open, and it is hoped that it will be possible to continue both to build on past relationships and to grow in fellowship in both Britain and Ireland.

14 BRITAIN AND IRELAND

The following proposals are based firmly on the principles elaborated by the 'Not Strangers But Pilgrims' process so far as they apply to the task of enabling the churches to seek more effective relationships and deepen unity at the level of Britain and Ireland. The proposals are put forward in the hope that they will serve the process by which the normal working of the churches will be enabled to grow into the unity the Holy Spirit is making possible.

The title for this instrument is to be

The Council of Churches for Britain and Ireland

1 Basis and Commitment

Basis
The Council of Churches for Britain and Ireland (formerly known as the British Council of Churches) is a fellowship of churches in the United Kingdom of Great Britain and Northern Ireland and in the Republic of Ireland which confess the Lord Jesus Christ as God and Saviour according to the Scriptures and therefore seek to fulfil their common calling to the glory of the one God, Father, Son and Holy Spirit.

Commitment
United in pilgrimage, these churches, in obedience to God's will and in the power of the Holy Spirit, commit themselves

to seek a deepening of their communion with Christ and with one another in the Church which is his body, and

to fulfil their mission to proclaim the Gospel by common witness and service in the world.

2 Objects, Aims and Purposes

a The objects of the Council of Churches for Britain and Ireland will be the advancement of the Christian religion, the relief of poverty and the advancement of education and any other purposes which are charitable according to the law of England and Wales.

b The Council will seek to further its objects by

i   providing a meeting place for churches in England, Ireland, Scotland and Wales, so that they may listen to and appreciate one another in their diversity and increasingly share their talents and traditions,

ii   holding together in appropriate ways the work of Churches Together in England, ACTS (Action of Churches Together in Scotland), Cytun (Churches Together in Wales), and Irish ecumenical bodies, and providing a point of reference for national and international inter-church agencies,

iii encouraging the churches to grow in the unity Christ gives and wills for his Church 'so that the world may believe',

iv   affirming and demonstrating the centrality of worship and prayer in all tasks undertaken,

v   enabling the churches to face together the matters that divide them so that they can grow into a fuller understanding of the nature, purpose and unity of Christ's Church,

vi   encouraging the churches to undertake together ventures in mission and evangelism,

vii enabling the churches to respond together to the needs of the human community, both in these islands and overseas, through the sharing of those resources which God provides,

viii enabling the churches to enter together into dialogue with the secular authorities in all appropriate matters,

ix   helping the churches to arrive at a common mind and make decisions together,

x   continuing to perform such functions and to discharge such responsibilities as have been given to or imposed upon the Council under its former name of the British Council of Churches and are deemed appropriate by the Council's member churches.

c   In all these matters the Council will mainly be concerned with those Church and public affairs that need the common resources, reflection or action of all the churches. In all such affairs the churches will keep in mind European and global dimensions.

3   Structure of the Council

We put forward, first and foremost, the essential elements of the Council which are all inter-related and inter-dependent. They are presented in the following paragraphs 4 to 7. Relationships between the churches in the

Council are through each and all of these. Ultimately authority for the Council is rooted in the decision-making bodies of the participating churches. Their different patterns of authority are reflected by the balance between the Church Representatives Meeting and the Assembly. Together they give direction to the Council and are the channels which the churches will use to decide which areas of work are needed and which have priority. Together they serve as the governing body of the Council of Churches for Britain and Ireland. This governing body constitutes the General Council of COCBI (as the legal successor to the BCC) as required by the Sharing of Church Buildings Act 1969. They will also be the means by which additional projects or areas of work will be agreed upon, and then financed or resourced in a variety of ways.

4 The Assembly

4.1 The Role of the Assembly

a The Assembly is an assembly of the churches, meeting every other year.

b The Assembly will be an occasion for deepening the relationships between the churches, for celebrating the gift of the unity we already enjoy and for seeking the fulness of that unity which can come from God alone. The timetable of the Assembly will be planned to ensure emphasis on shared prayer and worship.

c The Assembly will help to establish the direction and agenda of the Council for the next two years by reflecting, in an atmosphere of prayer and worship of God, on the needs of the world and the church, in the light of the previous undertakings of the churches.

d The Assembly will be able to hear the witness of Christians from other countries.

e The Assembly will deal with business raised by the member churches, the four national councils, the Church Representatives Meeting, the commissions and other agencies.

f As the Assembly considers the ecumenical tasks and opportunities for the future it may

   i   pass suggestions to the four national ecumenical bodies, and to the European or world ecumenical bodies;

   ii   affirm guidelines for the work of the Council itself;

   iii inform the member churches of common convictions;

   iv   make public statements for the Council.

g   When the Assembly acts under f.ii, the affirmations will be passed to the Steering Committee and the Church Representatives Meeting, so that practical implications may be discerned and the best way forward established.

h   The Assembly will receive information about the financing of the Council.

i   Responsibility for preparing the agenda and organising the Assembly will lie with the Steering Committee.

j   The Assembly will make such appointments as are provided for in other parts of this document.

4.2 Composition of the Assembly

a   The proposed pattern of membership (Schedule) is given below.

b   Those member churches who are also members of national ecumenical bodies are asked to ensure that approximately half of their Assembly representatives have been part of their churches' delegation to the relevant national ecumenical body.

c   Members of the Church Representatives Meeting are expected to be appointed to the Assembly by their churches.

d   The Assembly must seek to encompass the broader membership of the Christian community, while not losing its essential focus on churches. This is provided for in the proposed pattern of membership under the headings given there. When the Steering Committee allocates places in the Assembly for under-represented groups, having identified particular under-represented groups, it will confer with member churches and bodies in association to ensure that representatives of such groups are selected by member bodies of the Assembly, and are both fully part of their delegations and full members of the Assembly.

5   The Church Representatives Meeting

5.1 The Role of the Church Representatives Meeting

a   The Church Representatives Meeting will be an opportunity for those designated and recognised by their own churches as representatives to meet together regularly for prayer, discussion and study. It will have as its major concern the growth of visible unity and common mission in the life of the churches of Britain and Ireland.

b   The meetings will receive

i   declarations and affirmations from the Assembly;

ii   proposals, questions, comments from the member churches and from the four national ecumenical bodies;

iii proposals and papers from the ecumenical networks, commissions and agencies;

iv   materials from international dialogues and conferences.

c   The meeting will indicate how ecumenical work can be undertaken and when and how the resources of the churches can be brought into closer co-operation or united effort.

d   This meeting will be the point at which positions taken by the churches can be communicated to the Council, at which the Council as a corporate body may seek the approval of the churches to a specific line of action, and at which declarations of immediate public interest may be authorised as occasion demands.

e   The meeting will be responsible for the appointment of the Presidents of the Council (see 6 below).

f   The meeting will refer to the Steering Committee the detailed work on staffing, finance, organisation, implementation and management, so that it may concentrate on major issues of mission and unity. The meeting will receive periodic reports on this and will retain responsibility for making appointments of the General Secretary and Co-ordinating Secretaries, and for annual approval of the budget.

g   Meetings will take place two or three times a year, and will be serviced by the General Secretary of the Council. Meetings will be prepared by the Steering Committee.

5.2 Composition of Church Representatives Meeting

a   The meeting is composed of senior representatives appointed by the member churches or associations of churches.

b   The proposed allocation of places on the Church Representatives Meeting (Schedule) is given below.

c   The distribution of places proposed attempts to balance the need to give particular attention to the small churches while not ignoring the relative sizes of church membership.

d   Members of the Steering Committee will attend the Church Representatives Meeting with the right to speak.

e   The mind of the Meeting will not normally be discerned by voting but by reaching a broad consensus through prayer and deliberation.

6 Presidents of the Council

a   There will be six Presidents of the Council, each serving for four years, with three to be elected every two years by the Church Representatives Meeting.

b   The Presidents will be chosen to achieve, within the group of Presidents as a whole, balanced representation of church traditions and nations.

c   The Presidents will normally chair the various meetings of the Assembly and Church Representatives Meeting.

d   The Presidents may, as occasions demand, represent the Council in person on public occasions and will individually advocate the work of the Council.

7 Steering Committee

7.1 Role of the Steering Committee

a   To be the principal point of co-ordination and management for the work of the Council

   i   by receiving the results of Assembly meetings, Church Representatives Meetings, networks, commissions and agencies and taking forward the agreed initiatives through detailed arrangements between the churches and with the staff of the Council;

   ii   by drawing the attention of any part of the structure of the Council to matters being raised elsewhere within the Council or, in the opinion of the Committee, needing attention;

   iii   by being responsible for the detailed preparation of the Assemblies and Church Representatives Meetings.

b   To be the principal point of management of staffing and financing the Council

   i   by drawing up a co-ordinated budgeting procedure;

   ii   by taking responsibility for the management of resources and for all staff appointments except in the case of the General Secretary and Co-ordinating Secretaries which will be for nomination by the Committee to the Church Representatives Meeting.

c   The Steering Committee will meet at least nine times a year.

d   The Steering Committee will seek to express the 'service' and 'enabling' nature of the Council.

e   Members of the Steering Committee will attend the Church Representatives Meeting with the right to speak.

7.2 Composition of the Steering Committee

a   The Steering Committee will consist of
  −   six people appointed from and by the Church Representatives Meeting
  −   six people appointed from and by the Assembly
  −   a Chairperson appointed by the Church Representatives Meeting on the nomination of the Steering Committee
  −   the senior executive officer of each of the four national ecumenical bodies
  −   the General Secretary of the Council.

b   The six appointed by the Church Representatives Meeting will reflect the various Christian traditions.

c   The six appointed by the Assembly will reflect groups and interests which otherwise might be under-represented.

d   The Co-ordinating Secretaries of the Council will normally be expected to attend the Committee meetings; others may be invited to attend for specific business.

Schedule

The following is one possible membership schedule based on those who have been involved in the 'Not Strangers But Pilgrims' Process.

Ob = Observers at Swanwick   W = in Wales
E   = in England   I = in Ireland
S   = in Scotland

Name	Assembly Members	Representatives Meeting Associates/ Observers
African Methodist Episcopal Church	2	1
Afro West Indian United Council of Churches	2	1
Baptist Union of Gt. Britain	12	2
Baptist Union of Scotland	2	1

Baptist Union of Wales	2		1
Black Pastors' Conference		2	
Calvary Church of God in Christ	2		1
Cherubim and Seraphim	2		1
Church of England	45		4
Church of Ireland (Ob)	12		2
Church of Scotland	30		3
Church in Wales	8		1
Christian Bretheren	2		1
Congregational Federation EW	2		1
Congregational Union of Scotland	3		1
Council of African and Afro Caribbean Churches	3		1
Free Church Federal Council (for the smaller denominations)	2		1
Greek Orthodox	5		1
Independent Methodist	2		1
International Ministerial Council of Great Britain		2	
Lutheran Council	2		1
Methodist Church ESW	20		2
Methodist Church I (Ob)	3		1
Moravian Church EISW	2		1
New Testament Assembly	2		1
Oriental Orthodox	3		1
Presbyterian Church of Ireland (Ob)	12		2
Presbyterian Church of Wales	6		1
Religious Society of Friends ESW	3		1
Religious Society of Friends I (Ob)	2		1
Roman Catholic EW	40		4
Roman Catholic S	20		2
Russian Orthodox	2		1
Salvation Army	5		1
Scottish Episcopal Church	3		1
Shiloh United Church of Christ	2		1
Union of Welsh Independents	5		1
United Free Church of Scotland	2		1
United Reformed Church ESW	12		2
Unitarians		2	
Wesleyan Holiness Church	2		1
West Indian Evangelical Alliance		2	

Bodies in Association	15		
Regional Ecumenical Reps		15	
For allocation to under-represented groups	25		
General Secretaries of the national bodies, General Secretary of COCBI and representatives of Agencies as defined in this report.	10		
	336	23	52

Overall Total of Assembly: 359

Overall Total of Church Representatives Meeting (including attending Steering Committee members): 63

8 Patterns of Work and Staffing

8.1 Introduction

a   The Inter-Church Meeting has received, alongside the responses of the churches, a large number of papers and suggestions from all sorts of groups presently involved in common Christian work (see note below). We are grateful to have been entrusted with all this and gladly affirm that much of what we have read is impressive, significant and promising for the future. And yet it is also clear that many people are in danger of expecting too much from us.

b   It cannot be part of the purpose of the Inter-Church Process to evaluate each of the pieces of work involved and to 'tidy up' this complex scene into any single pattern to be put into effect in 1990. That task would be well beyond our competence. More important, we believe it would be wrong to attempt it, since it will be for the churches which form the new COCBI to decide which pieces of work they wish to pursue and through what specific instruments. Much of that deciding will best be carried out within the committed fellowship of the new Councils; in what follows we are trying to limit our recommendations to areas in which decisions need to be taken in 1989/90.

c   In particular we are aware of vital responsibilities that the member churches of the BCC have taken on in the work currently being done by the BCC and which should not be downgraded or damaged by inadequate consideration at this stage of the process. We are concerned to put recommendations to the churches that can in appropriate ways *both* safeguard continuity for important existing work *and* provide room for development.

d   The broad outlines that follow take forward the proposals in the interim report and are intended to provide the skeleton through which the ecumenical activities may be articulated. The more detailed provisions for major pieces of work are offered as the necessary constitutional bridge from existing structures to the new. The churches through the new councils will be in a position within a year or two to adapt and amend these structures as the common experience develops. The list in Appendix I then provides an overview of those other existing or developing activities which may be continued if the churches so decide and if the appropriate support is made available.

Note:
A vast range of activity has been pursued under the auspices of the British Council of Churches and of its five Divisional Boards; this was mapped out succinctly in the 75 full pages of the Survey of BCC Work presented to the BCC Assembly in 1987. The large number of commissions, standing committees and working groups listed there work alongside a great many comparable bodies; some of the latter, like the Joint Liturgical Group or the Churches' Council for Health and Healing, have no constitutional relation to the BCC. They are constituted by representatives officially appointed and paid for by churches, and have informal relations with the Council. Others, for example the Student Christian Movement and the National Association of Christian Communities and Networks, do not seek to work 'under' the denominations but maintain close links and are centrally concerned that their work reflect and serve the uniting impetus of the Holy Spirit.

8.2 Britain/Ireland and the four national ecumenical bodies

a   The Swanwick Report (p. 25) spoke, in a way that has earned wide assent, of developing 'complementary agendas . . . so that both levels of instruments would be part of an integrated operation with an agreed division of labour.' Yet it has not proved easy to determine criteria for suggesting with any precision how the tasks should be divided up. A great deal will have to be decided in the early years of the life of the new bodies, and by providing for the presence of the five General Secretaries in both the Church Representatives Meeting and the Steering Committee of COCBI we trust that they will have this concern constantly before them.

b   In general we suggest:

i   that most matters to do with the support and encouragement of the ecumenical movement at the primary local level and at the intermediate or regional level of church life be entrusted to the four national bodies;

ii   that matters of common responsibility of the British and Irish churches in international affairs and relationships be entrusted to COCBI;

iii that in the wider range of public affairs and of communications responsibility will need to be sensibly shared between the two levels, with COCBI concerned for what concerns all the churches and yet seeking to recognise, in terms of 'subsidiarity', that as far as possible responsibility and initiative rest with the national bodies.

8.3 The principles involved

The future pattern of work and staffing will be guided by the following four general principles:

a **Owning the common work.** The crucial step decided at the 1987 Swanwick Conference is encapsulated in the phrase: 'from co-operation to commitment'. This indicates that what goes on within and through the COCBI must no longer be an 'optional extra' for the churches, over and above what they do through their 'own' separate working structures. It must be, much more clearly, that which the churches do together, drawing on whatever resources the Holy Spirit provides and evokes within any of them. Too often in the past the councils of churches have served as an 'alibi' for the churches, allowing a relatively small number of people to pursue pieces of work in the name of the churches yet which the churches have been entirely free to overlook or repudiate when they so wish. By the same token there has been the lack of direct answerability to the churches. The step into commitment needs to be expressed in working patterns which the churches will see as their own and which more centrally and effectively engage the life of each church.

b **Both continuity and openness to the future.** The new working patterns must build on the best of what has developed over the years. There is general eagerness to see all the strengths of the earlier bodies carried on into the new patterns. At the same time the COCBI must not simply be a copy or an extension of what has been; there must be a real freedom to imagine new possibilities that express the new commitment in a constantly changing context, and therefore a genuine measure of flexibility.

c **Oriented to the essential task.** Conferences and committees must not be called into being for their own sake but to serve a task that is seen to be inherent in the calling of the Church. The working patterns of the COCBI must be such as to anticipate and encourage the growth of separated churches into a truer expression of Christ's Body, the Church.

d **On pilgrimage.** Any set of working patterns that can be put forward now should not be expected to last unchanged for more than ten years. We therefore suggest that the COCBI be committed to making a full review of its life and work in 1997/8 with the expectation of revising what came into being in 1990 in time for the 21st century.

8.4 Staffing

In order to carry through these principles into the life of the Council there will be both a 'core' staff which is directly engaged by the churches as they work together in the Council, and a whole range of other resources to be used in a variety of ways which are described in the following sections.

a   **The core staff of the Council**

i   The core staff will consist of a General Secretary and four Co-ordinating Secretaries, with appropriate administrative and secretarial assistance, and with the necessary financial and other services shared, as appropriate, with other bodies in Inter-Church House. All these posts will be open to women as well as men; the Council will intend to be an equal opportunities employer.

ii   The General Secretary will be responsible for ensuring that the policies which are set by the Assembly, Church Representatives Meeting and Steering Committee are carried through. The General Secretary will develop and review patterns of teamwork and shared responsibility among the core staff of agencies and commissions.

iii   The Co-ordinating Secretaries will have oversight of the four areas of work set out below. They will have broad areas of concern assigned to them, but not so as to take executive responsibility for any specific group or piece of work. They are to give their time to 'oversight' of what is and is not being done through the churches, associated bodies, the four national councils and other relevant groupings. They will seek the better co-ordination of effort and the stimulation and exploration of what might be better done and how it could be better done. As such ideas become clear and agreed so it will be a vital part of their task, under the guidance of the Steering Committee and Church Representatives Meeting, to imagine and suggest which patterns of work would be appropriate and how the necessary budget could be raised. They are not to be tied down with the obligation of administering several working groups and a sub-stantial budget of 'their own', but rather to be deliberately set free to explore where the priorities for Christian obedience now are and how they can best be served.

iv   Each Co-ordinating Secretary will be expected to gather, in consultation with the Steering Committee, an informal group of not more than 12 persons drawn from several churches who can guide and support her/him in the whole area to which oversight is to be given.

b Areas of our Common Task

The four broad areas of work are these. They are to be viewed in the light of paragraphs 8.2 and 8.3 above. In listing them like this we stress the need to allow for a flexibility of approach, since no one area is wholly distinct from the others, since complementary patterns of working with the four national councils need to be worked out, and since the experience and gifts of particular staff members – in the ecumenical bodies and in the churches – must be deployed as efficiently as possible.

i Church Life

In this area the four national bodies will be carrying the primary responsibility for inter-church relationships, but there will remain considerable issues to be faced by all the churches together. Among these are likely to be: the theological questions of Christian unity; relating Christian faith to a changing and plural society; the renewal of worship and spirituality; the varied needs for theological education; the role of women, lay members and young people; the challenge of mission and evangelism; the development of ecumenical communities, and making and developing contact with Christians not in relation with member bodies of the Council.

ii Public Involvement

This area has to do with the questions of contemporary society, for instance the whole economic order of industry, commerce and all forms of wealth creation; the world of work; the future of the welfare state; the patterns of democracy and of social cohesion; matters of housing, employment and education; privilege and deprivation; the place of young people, of women and of the elderly in society; race and inter-ethnic relations, and current questions of social and personal morality.

iii World Context

This area has to do with the wider international relationships of churches and secular communities in Britain and Ireland and the pressures by which so much of our life is affected: the tensions between a richer North and a poorer South; international rivalries and conflicts; the ecological questions that call for international co-operation; serving the needs of refugees, migrants and those whose rights are violated; the development of the UNO and other international institutions. (See also the proposed Commission on Mission, section 9 below).

iv Communications

This area has to do with the questions of a world increasingly dependent upon rapid and reliable information and dominated by powerful systems and means of communication, the developing patterns of communication between the churches themselves and between the churches and society at large, and the promotion through appropriate media of the common work of the churches through these councils. It is recognised that this is a dimension of all the life and working of the new ecumenical bodies.

c **Finance**

The costs of this core staff are provided for in the 'enabling' budget set out in Appendix 3. This is deliberately limited to those members of staff and patterns of work which are seen as necessary for the effective running of the representative structures and the work of the Co-ordinating Secretaries.

8.5 Three main patterns of work

a   The Swanwick Conference, our preceding reports and many of the papers we have received have made clear that different patterns of work will be needed to fulfil our commitment as churches. We propose that these be seen in three categories:

i   a body which can act simply as a *co-ordinator*, not doing its own work but providing its services to bring representatives of the churches together to exchange views and experiences and to explore their own agreements and disagreements. Many of the standing bodies linked with COCBI will be of this sort, *NETWORKS* of persons with similar mandates and concerns in the various churches and associated bodies.

ii   a body which can act *on behalf of* the members churches, bringing together some of the specialists from the member churches or even representatives of some of their specialist committees, so that together they may pool their experience and insight. This does not replace similar work in the member churches, but rather is intended to complement it and to be fed into the member churches through their own agencies or groups working in the same field. Such *COMMISSIONS* may be established as relatively long-term, to give continuing oversight over a wide area, or as relatively short-term, to investigate or think through a particular challenge and hand back responsibility for the follow-up of their work to the churches which requested it.

iii   a body which can act *instead of* the member churches through agencies which act ecumenically in a way which means that the member churches do not need their own parallel machinery. The obvious example of this is Christian Aid. These may be termed *AGENCIES*. Other examples of bodies appointed by the churches and which do the work in such a way that churches see it as their own at present include, in the BCC Division of Community Affairs, the BCC Community and Race Relations Unit, the Community Work Resource Agency and the Opportunities for Volunteering scheme, and, in the Conference for World Mission, the groups handling relations with China.

iv We have considered how these various patterns may be most helpfully related to the representative bodies of COCBI. This is a matter which will develop with the experience and life of the Council. Initially we propose as follows:

- each church should make its own internal arrangements for its representatives in the various networks, commissions and agencies to which it commits itself to report back and consult on their mandate;

- the Church Representatives Meeting will ask one of its members to stay in touch with each of these groupings and feed back important findings or dilemmas;

- each network/commission/agency should establish contact with at least one member of the Assembly who can be kept knowledgeable about its work and encouraged to speak for it on occasion;

- the General Secretary and Co-ordinating Secretaries of COCBI will in teamwork agree on a pattern of contact between themselves and these groupings, and will encourage appropriate consultation, team-work and cross-fertilisation.

b   Resources and Finance

The resourcing of these patterns of work will need to be appropriate to the character of the commitment involved, and may be described as follows:

i In the case of NETWORKS there will be no 'separate' staff person assigned to them; one or other of the networks' own number will be elected to act for a time as chair/secretary/treasurer in whatever functions the network decides it neeeds, with any common budget being brought together by pooling by the member bodies;

ii In the case of COMMISSIONS the whole matter of the staff time needed and of the budget for their work must be thought out in the early stages of planning and agreed by the churches. If one or more full-time staff persons needs to be assigned, such (a) person(s) would have to be released from existing obligations and financed with the agreement of the churches participating in the Commission. For this reason the budget here out-lined for COCBI does not include financial provision for possible Commissions.

iii   In the case of AGENCIES these can only operate and employ staff when their budget is sufficiently ensured, whether by their own fund-raising or by pledges of the necessary support from appropriate quarters.

9   Particular Areas of Work

Christian Aid

1   We are grateful to Christian Aid for submitting a paper setting out its own hopes for its future. We have tried to take full account of it. Christian Aid belongs to the member churches of the British Council of Churches. It was created by them and it is responsible ultimately to them. It enables those churches to act and make their response together to the gifts and demands of the world's poor. We confirm Christian Aid in its task as expressed in *The Task of Christian Aid* (1981) and *To Strengthen the Poor* (1987).

2   We recommend that Christian Aid retain its independent charitable status; that the Director and staff be responsible to a Board for the work of Christian Aid; and that the Board comprise:

(a)   A Moderator (see para 5 below).

(b)   16 members appointed by the member Churches who sponsor Christian Aid. Each sponsoring Church will be entitled to put forward candidates for membership of the Board. Those members of the COCBI Church Representatives Meeting, who have been appointed by Churches which sponsor Christian Aid, will decide how these 16 members are then chosen. In so doing they will ensure that the larger sponsoring Churches are always represented, and the smaller ones represented in rotation; they will ensure that there is a community of women and men, young and old, ordained and lay, as well as geographical spread in the membership; they will attempt to ensure a balance of appropriate knowledge and skills for the task.

(c)   the General Secretary of COCBI.

(d)   4 members, one nominated by each of the national ecumenical bodies.

(e)   5 members co-opted for special knowledge or skills.

3   The Board is encouraged to appoint consultants from third world countries, as well as other consultants and observers as appropriate.

4   Co-operation between the development agencies (Christian Aid, Methodist Relief Fund, Catholic Fund for Overseas Development, Scottish Catholic International Aid Fund, Tear Fund and Trocaire) already

well developed, should now enter a new phase. The commitment expressed by the churches at Swanwick calls for the closest co-operation between these agencies, producing the best possible service and witness.

5   Those members of the COCBI Church Representatives' Meeting who have been appointed by churches which sponsor Christian Aid will appoint the Board's Moderator, preferably from among the members of the Church Representatives Meeting. The Moderator will be an advocate for Christian Aid and an immediate support for the Director.

6   The Board will appoint a Director and other senior staff as may be agreed.

7   Members of the Board and its Moderator will serve for a period of four years, renewable for one such further period.

8   The Board will appoint such committees and other officers as are required.

9   The Board will send an annual report of its work to each of the sponsoring churches, who will be responsible for seeing that Christian Aid's work is known and reviewed in appropriate ways in its own constituency.

10   The Board will send an annual report of its work to COCBI. Sponsoring churches who wish to raise matters concerning Christian Aid's work or constitution are encouraged to do so both directly in the Board and in the COCBI Assembly. Any changes in the constitutional framework of Christian Aid will require the written agreement of the appropriate authorities of at least two-thirds of the sponsoring churches. Such changes should normally be discussed first in the COCBI Assembly or in the Church Representatives Meeting.

Churches' Commission on Mission

1   There has been a long, intimate and complex association between councils of churches and mission agencies. In the United Kingdom and Ireland this has taken shape in the Conference for World Mission (formerly the Conference of British Missionary Societies) as a Division of The British Council of Churches which has its own membership and financing. Major developments in this generation require a flexible approach at this point. The world mission agencies which are members of the Conference for World Mission, together with their counterparts in the (Roman Catholic) National Missionary Council, seek ways of helping the churches to fulfil their intention of recognising mission as central to their ecumenical purpose. The agencies' historic involvement overseas is a reminder that mission was once seen as an overseas activity, and now must be replaced by commitment to one mission

in one world. We are grateful to the Conference for World Mission and the National Missionary Council for the joint submission of their views.

2   The agencies' particular contribution concerns the global dimension of mission, and is directed to enabling the churches in Britain to participate more fully in that mission. This contribution can be made in two principal ways:

(a)   First, the mission agencies and development agencies have a great deal to contribute to the international responsibilities of the British and Irish churches.

(b)   Secondly, through the Commission on Mission the agencies can bring insights and experience gained in other parts of the world to the work of mission in Britain and Ireland.

3   It is proposed that from 1990 an organically related body of the Council of Churches for Britain and Ireland will be the

Churches' Commission on Mission

Its remit will be:

(a)   To provide a forum for sharing information and for mutual encouragement in the area of evangelism at home and overseas.

(b)   To enable the experience of churches overseas to illuminate and assist the missionary calling in these islands.

(c)   To assist the churches in the educational task of relating local and global witness and service.

(d)   To consider the theological issues of Christian witness in a divided world and a secular culture.

(e)   To enable the churches to respond together when opportunities arise for joint witness and service in churches throughout the world.

(f)   To relate to international bodies concerned with mission and evangelism.

4   It is recommended:

that the member churches of the Council of Churches for Britain and Ireland will be members of the Churches' Commission on Mission unless a church expressly declines such membership.

that the full meeting of the Commission, not less than once a year, comprises representatives of the churches totalling approximately 75.

that the Commissioning Body to be appointed by the present Inter-Church Meeting should settle the precise number of members that each church should have on the Commission ranging from one up to 12 from the largest church. There will also be representatives of non-denominational mission agencies and the four national ecumenical bodies. Each church will arrange that its delegation includes people who represent the mission agencies associated with that church.

that the Commission appoint its own Standing Committee of not more than 15 people to deal with business between meetings of the Commission.

5 It is proposed that the Council of Churches for Britain and Ireland Co-ordinating Secretaries act as Advisers to the Commission as appropriate, with a particular care for inter-church relationships.

It is proposed that the Divisional Secretary of the Conference for World Mission be the Organising Secretary of the Commission, technically employed by CFWM.

It is proposed that CFWM indicate initially what other posts, both for executive and support staff, will be needed and supported by them, and that after a few years the Commission will review staffing with the possibility that the Commission itself become the employing body.

6 It is proposed that the continuing office of CFWM be at Inter-Church House.

7 Since the four national ecumenical bodies will have a primary care for evangelism and joint outreach in the four nations and a general concern for the overall mission of the church, it will be important that they are well represented in the life and work of the Commission. The aim is that the Commission should become the key point of interchange, with national ecumenical bodies, international bodies and mission agencies all helping the churches to fulfil their missionary calling.

8 The Conference for World Mission, a legal body, with its own member-ship and charitable status, is likely to continue beyond 1990 and it is recom-mended that its major contribution to ecumenical life be through the Commission, which will replace the Divisional Board. At 1990 its budget will separate from the Council of Churches for Britain and Ireland. As the Commission on Mission becomes established, we expect that the responsibilities of CWFM will gradually and progressively be transferred to it.

Other Agencies

There is a particular responsibility for certain agencies and activities which at present are integral to the British Council of Churches and which might cease by default in 1990 unless we take action now.

Our problem is that the ultimate decision about the continuity of this work should be taken by the Council of Churches for Britain and Ireland; but if a decision is left until 1990 then it will be too late to maintain what is of value in the existing work.

We therefore make recommendations about three specific pieces of work. We propose temporary bridging arrangements to enable the current work to continue for as long as it is necessary for COCBI to evaluate it, and to decide whether to keep it as it is, to change it or to close it down.

A   The Committee for Relations with People of Other Faiths

1   In response to an Assembly Resolution of the British Council of Churches in 1977, the Committee for Relations with People of Other Faiths (CRPOF) was established as a distinct unit within the general orbit of the Conference for World Mission. A full-time executive secretary was appointed. CRPOF was commissioned to

act as an ecumenical instrument to assist churches and mission agencies to help Christians both to learn from those of other faiths and to bear witness to their own faith,

help clarify Christian conviction and promote theological reflection on faith to faith relationships, the plural society and, in these contexts, the missionary calling.

CRPOF was also mandated to liaise between denominational committees concerned with interfaith relations, to monitor and initiate 'creative faith to faith engagement by the churches'.

CRPOF has the active participation of Roman Catholic observers.

2   Several churches now have their own committees for relations with people of other faiths, some with part-time staff. All of these try to work closely with CRPOF. There are also several specialist interfaith agencies (two in Selly Oak), and a fledgling Inter-Faith Network.

3   CRPOF was inaugurated with finance provided by the mission agencies and overseas mission departments of the member churches of the British Council of Churches. Its present finance comes from three sources:

(a) £15,000 from the mission agencies and overseas mission departments
(b) £5,000 from a trust fund
(c) £5,000 from the main budget of the BCC (provided by the member churches).

The mission agencies are hoping that in future the full financial support of CRPOF should come on the main budget provided by the member churches.

4   We recommend that CRPOF continue for the time being to be accountable

to the CFWM Board or to the Commission on Mission when it is established, until such time as the Church Representatives Meeting shall have had the opportunity to review its work and to make recommendations to the churches about its future.

B The Community and Race Relations Unit (CRRU)

5   The Swanwick Conference was 'painfully aware of the divisions between . . . black and white'. It was also 'heartened' by 'the full participation in this Process of the Black-led churches'. There is no question but that the churches in Britain and Ireland will wish to work together for the improvement of race relations. However, the churches themselves must decide, when COCBI is established, how precisely they wish to do this work.

6   Until they are able to make that decision we propose that the Community and Race Relations Unit, at present within the Division of Community affairs of the BCC, should continue. CRRU already has its own Board and we propose that this continues to oversee the work until the churches together decide upon its future. In the event of the Division of Community Affairs ceasing to exist we propose that the CRRU Board be answerable to the COCBI Church Representatives Meeting through the Steering Committee and the General Secretary.

7   CRRU at present has two full-time and one half-time executive staff members. At present the equivalent of the salary and expenses of one full-time post is met by the main budget of the BCC from the contributions of member churches. The cost of the half-time post comes from a trust fund, and three special grants meet the cost of the other full-time post.

C Opportunities for Volunteering

8   Opportunities for Volunteering carries on a self-contained operation at present within the BCC Division of Community Affairs. It is totally funded from Government sources.

9   We propose that this operation, including its advisory group and staffing arrangements, should continue beyond 1990 until the churches shall have evaluated it and made a decision about its future. Until that decision is made and from 1990 it should be supervised by the Church Representatives' Meeting through the General Secretary and Steering Committee of COCBI.

D Financing Continuing Agencies

Christian Aid and CFWM are self-financing bodies.

Opportunities for Volunteering is totally funded from Government sources. CRPOF and CRRU will require some funding from church sources, if they are to continue even for a limited period. In the paragraphs above we have outlined the sources of their present funding. We hope the trusts and agencies which have funded them hitherto will continue to do so. If this should prove not to be the case, then we believe that any shortfall should be met for a limited period of not moe than two years as a first claim on any financial resources made available from the British Council of Churches.

10 Young People and Women's Concerns

1   Women and young people are not segments of Church work in the same way as development and aid agencies, race relations, economic or international affairs. Women and young people are living members of the Church and of society, therefore all the work of all the ecumenical instruments is relevant to them.

2   Nevertheless the Swanwick Conference recognised that young people and women were under-represented both at the Conference and generally at meetings where the churches make major decisions about their life and work. The *Swanwick Report* noted that ecumenical 'instruments will need . . . to allow sufficient representation by young people at every level possible' (p. 14). Moreover, we are at the beginning of the World Council of Churches' Ecumenical Decade – Churches in Solidarity with Women. How should the churches together provide resources to enable young people and women to play their full and proper part in the life and work of the churches and society, and especially of the ecumenical movement in Great Britain and Ireland, and to ensure that their concerns are adequately heard?

3   We are confident that the churches will wish to have an item on the central budget sufficient to encourage and enable young people and women to participate fully in the churches' ecumenical work and witness. We recommend that 15% be added to the rest of the working budget of COCBI for these purposes.

4   We are grateful to the BCC Youth Unit Reference Group for their paper. More discussion, however, is needed about their proposals, and in particular the relationship of the youth bodies to the representative councils of COCBI. Therefore until the churches working through COCBI have decided on the means by which this should be done, we recommend that the BCC Youth Unit continue in its present form with one executive staff person paid for by the main

contributions of the churches, and, if possible, with a second post paid for by the Department of Education and Science. We recommend that when the Division of Ecumenical Affairs of the BCC ceases in 1990, that the Youth Unit and its Reference Group be responsible to the Church Representatives Meeting of COCBI through the Steering Committee and the General Secretary.

5   We are grateful to the Women's Interchurch Consultative Committee for their paper and recommendations. We consider that further discussion is needed, in particular to clarify the location of a full-time staff person in relation to COCBI. We recommend that the churches and the Church Representatives Meeting should engage with the Women's Interchurch Consultative Committee about the future organisation of this work.

Appendix 1

As mentioned in section 8 of the above report the various groupings in which the churches will work together in the COCBI need to be seen in different categories. Here is a list of possible groupings that the churches considering membership of COCBI and the sister councils may wish to work through; all the items here have been spelt out in one or other of the papers made available to the Inter-Church Meeting (especially the 1987 *Survey of BCC Work* and the 1988 *BCC Responses*, to which page numbers refer) to which reference should be made for the details. It depends on the ways in which the churches will wish to structure the work whether these are best seen as networks, commissions or agencies. We have not set out this list under those headings, but it begins with those which are clearly networks and ends with those best seen as agencies. We include the suggested staffing put forward in the papers we have received. Please note that there is otherwise no particular priority suggested by the order, and that the names here used are simply those convenient for reference, not suggested titles.

Stewardship Officers (page 60)

Education Officers (pages 75 and 95)

Women's Inter-Church Network (page 32)
>   A co-ordinating secretary for women's concerns and the community of women and men in the Church is widely seen as a priority, and provided for by an allocation on the 'enabling' budget. (See Section 10 above)

Youth Inter-Church Network (page 26)
>   Two executive secretaries and support staff are requested, along with two biennial internships for the Chair and Secretary of the Four Nations

Ecumenical Youth Assembly. An allocation on the 'enabling' budget provides the essential starting-point – (see Section 10 above)

Standing Committee on Theological Education (page 57)

The Theology of Christian Unity (page 52)

Unity in Prayer (page 42)

Collaborative Ministry (page 60)

Social Responsibility (page 66)

Economics and the World of Work (page 65 and the paper: B30 submitted by the Churches' Consortium on Industrial Mission, in which it is suggested that the necessary finance and staff time could develop from those presently made available to the CCIM.)

International Affairs, with sub-groups on particular areas and concerns (page 97) Particular staff members are available at present, thanks to grants from missionary agencies and trusts, for Asia, for Africa and for Peace and Human Rights.

Relations with People of Other Faiths (page 91)
A full-time staff member with secretarial assistance and a work budget – see Section 9 above.

Community and Race Relations (page 73)
Two full-time and one half-time staff members with 2 Admin. Assistants are at present serving this vital unit – see Section 9.

China Relationships and Study Project (page 85)
One executive and one administrative staff members serve at present, under a special budget of the Conference for World Mission.

Mission Partners Committees for South India, North India, Pakistan and Bangladesh (page 85)
Served by the Asia Secretary of CFWM, these co-ordinate relationships between the united churches of the Indian sub-continent, the British churches and several European and N. American churches.

Community Work Resource Agency (page 70)
Looks to a 'basic level of staffing and administrative capacity'.

Opportunities for Volunteering (page 63)
A full-time staff post for as long as the DHSS is prepared to fund it.

Commission on Mission, with bodies for Partnership in Evangelism in the 4 nations (pages 46 and 85)
Two executive staff in COCBI, devoted respectively to the global and local dimensions of mission – see Section 9.

Christian Aid (page 77)
    Director and a large team of staff – see Section 9.

Appendix 2

This lists other bodies supported by two or more churches, which have played important parts in the total ecumenical movement in Britain and Ireland and which are to be kept in mind. Where a body has itself submitted a paper on its future work and relationships we indicate that. This list is not intended to be taken as complete or as anything more than a provisional list. It is in no particular order.

Free Church Federal Council (B7)
Churches' Council for Health and Healing (B31)
Churches' Commission on Overseas Students (B19)
National Ecumenical Agency in Further Eduction
Christian Education Movement
Consultative Group on Ministry among Children (B34)
Conference on Adult and Continuing Education
Association of Centres of Adult Theological Eduction (B23)
Theological Education by Extension Forum (B26)
Joint Education Policy Committee
Family Life Ecumenical Education Project
Churches' Council on Alcohol and Drugs
National Christian Education Council
Joint Liturgical Group
Conference for Christian Partnership (B8)
Christians Against Racism and Fascism
Christian Enquiry Agency (England/Scotland)
Christians Abroad (B12)
Christian Concern for Southern Africa
Churches' Committee of the World Development Movement
Action by Christians Against Torture (B14)
Church Action on Poverty
Church Action with the Unemployed
Church Action on Disability
Joint Committee for Hospital Chaplaincies
Associations of Church Communication Officers (B39)
Churches' Advisory Committee for Local Broadcasting (B4)
Council on Christian Approaches to Defence and Disarmament
Churches' Consortium on Industrial Mission (B30)
Churches' Main Committee
Association for Christian Communication

British Churches Committee for Channel 4
Church Action for Central America
Churches' Television and Radio Centre
Association of Inter-Church Families

The B numbers refer to submissions made by these bodies to the Inter-Church
Process.

Appendix 3

Preliminary Budget for COCBI

Staff Costs, including NI and Superannuation

		£	£
General Secretary		22,000	
4 Co-ordinating Secretaries	at 18,850	75,400	
4 clerical, senior	at 12,350	49,400	
3 clerical, junior	at 10,400	31,200	178,000

Working Costs

Office facilities at Inter-Church House, equipment depreciation and maintenance, stationery	35,000	
Share in admin. and finance services	24,000	
Committee costs	5,000	
Staff Travel	7,000	
Postage and Telephone	7,500	
Share of printing/bookshop facility	15,000	
Assistance to Networks	5,000	
Contingencies	5,000	103,500

Support for Youth Secretary and office	22,500	
Support for Women's Concerns office	20,000	42,500
		£324,000

Bridging finance for CRRU and CRPOF
to be sought.

15 PARTICIPANTS AND OBSERVERS

Churches and Associations of Churches participating in the Inter-Church Process 1985 - 1989

African Methodist Episcopal Church
Afro-West Indian United Council of Churches
Baptist Union of Great Britain
Baptist Union of Wales
Black Pastors' Conference
Calvary Church of God in Christ
Cherubim and Seraphim Council of Churches
Church in Wales
Church of England
Church of Scotland
Congregational Federation
Congregational Union of Scotland
Council of African and Afro-Caribbean Churches
Council of Oriental Orthodox Christian Churches
Countess of Huntingdon's Connexion
Greek Orthodox Church
Independent Methodist Church
International Ministerial Council of Great Britain
Lutheran Council of Great Britain
Methodist Church
Moravian Church
New Testament Assembly
Presbyterian Church of Wales
Religious Society of Friends
Roman Catholic Church in England and Wales
Roman Catholic Church in Scotland
Russian Orthodox Church
Salvation Army
Scottish Episcopal Church
Union of Welsh Independents
Unitarian Church
United Free Church of Scotland
United Reformed Church
Wesleyan Holiness Church

Baptist Union of Scotland
British Council of Churches
Christian Aid
Christian Brethren
Church of Ireland
Council of Churches for Wales
Fellowship of Churches of Christ
Free Church Federal Council
Irish Council of Churches
Irish Inter-Church Meeting ('Ballymascanlon')
Methodist Church in Ireland
National Centre for Christian Communities and Networks
Presbyterian Church in Ireland
Scottish Churches Council
Seventh Day Adventists
Student Christian Movement
West Indian Evangelical Alliance
Young Men's Christian Association
Young Women's Christian Association

16 THE PROPOSED ECUMENICAL STRUCTURES

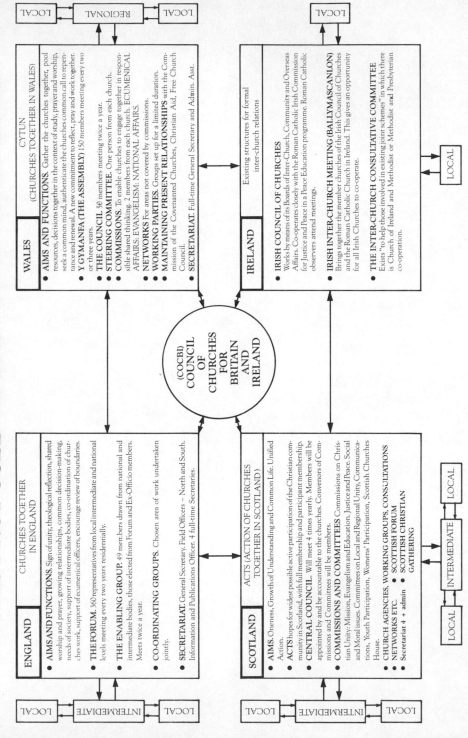

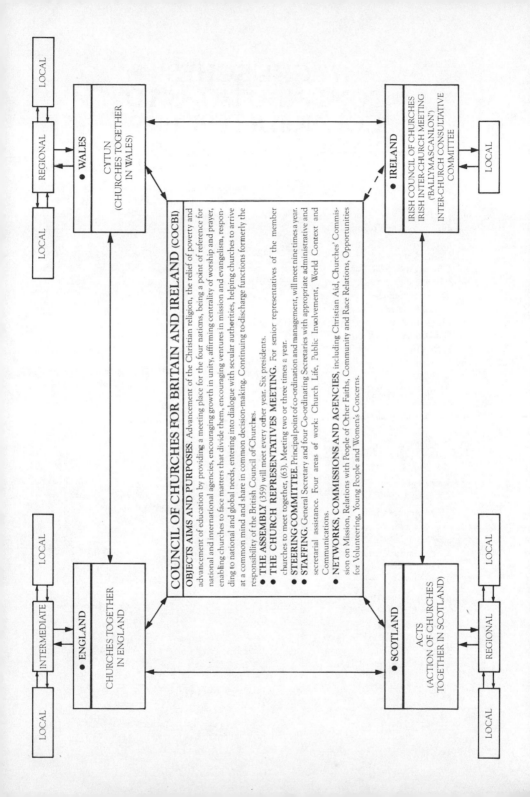

COUNCIL OF CHURCHES FOR BRITAIN AND IRELAND (COCBI)

OBJECTS AIMS AND PURPOSES. Advancement of the Christian religion, the relief of poverty and advancement of education by providing a meeting place for the four nations, being a point of reference for national and international agencies, encouraging growth in unity, affirming centrality of worship and prayer, enabling churches to face matters that divide them, encouraging ventures in mission and evangelism, responding to national and global needs, entering into dialogue with secular authorities, helping churches to arrive at a common mind and share in common decision-making. Continuing to discharge functions formerly the responsibility of the British Council of Churches.

- **THE ASSEMBLY** (359) will meet every other year. Six presidents.
- **THE CHURCH REPRESENTATIVES MEETING.** For senior representatives of the member churches to meet together, (63). Meeting two or three times a year.
- **STEERING COMMITTEE.** Principal point of co-ordination and management, will meet nine times a year.
- **STAFFING.** General Secretary and four Co-ordinating Secretaries with appropriate administrative and secretarial assistance. Four areas of work: Church Life, Public Involvement, World Context and Communications.
- **NETWORKS, COMMISSIONS AND AGENCIES,** including Christian Aid, Churches' Commission on Mission, Relations with People of Other Faiths, Community and Race Relations, Opportunities for Volunteering, Young People and Women's Concerns.

● **WALES**
CYTUN
(CHURCHES TOGETHER
IN WALES)

LOCAL — REGIONAL — LOCAL

● **IRELAND**
IRISH COUNCIL OF CHURCHES
IRISH INTER-CHURCH MEETING
('BALLYMASCANLON')
INTER-CHURCH CONSULTATIVE
COMMITTEE

LOCAL

● **ENGLAND**
CHURCHES TOGETHER
IN ENGLAND

LOCAL — INTERMEDIATE — LOCAL

● **SCOTLAND**
ACTS
(ACTION OF CHURCHES
TOGETHER IN SCOTLAND)

LOCAL — REGIONAL — LOCAL

17 CHURCHES' CONTRIBUTIONS TO COUNCILS FOR 1989

Church	BCC	Scottish Churches Council	Council of Churches for Wales	Total
Headquarters in England	£	£	£	£
African Methodist Episcopal				
Baptist Union	19,640			19,640
Cherubim & Seraphim				
Church of England	213,950			213,950
Congregational Federation	608			608
Council of African and A-C Churches				
Greek Orthodox				
Independent Methodist	570			570
International Ministerial Council of GB	58			58
Lutheran	1,100			1,100
Methodist	52,975	640	2,976*	56,591
Moravian	330			330
Oriental Orthodox				
Russian Orthodox	515			515
Salvation Army	1,100	245	248	1,593
Shiloh United Church of Christ				
Society of Friends	4,145	85		4,230
Unitarian	678			678
United Reformed Church	28,710	90	948*	29,784
Headquarters in Scotland				
Baptist Union of Scotland	548	1,030		1,578
Church of Scotland	68,398	43,115		111,513
Congregational Union of Scotland	1,280	1,385		2,665
Scottish Episcopal Church	7,177	6,295		13,472
United Free Church	727	700		1,427
Headquarters in Wales				
Baptist Union of Wales [1]			2,384	2,384
Church in Wales	9,022		15,472*	24,494
Presbyterian Church of Wales	857		9,528*	10,385
Union of Welsh Independents	331		3,600	3,931
Baptist Union of GB Churches in Wales			960*	960
		53,585	36,152	

Headquarters in Ireland[2]

Church in Ireland	9,560	9,560
Methodist Church in Ireland	1,644	1,644
Presbyterian Church in Ireland	4,877	4,877
	428,800	518,537

* These figures include an amount for the Commission of Covenanted Churches in Wales.

[1] The Baptist Union of Wales is not a member body of BCC.

[2] Since future relationships of churches in Ireland have not yet been settled the contributions to the Irish Council of Churches are not included.

18 NOTE ON OVERALL BUDGET

1   Each of the working parties attempted an outline budget for the new bodies as they will be in the 1991 full accounting year, and these attempts are included in the main report. The Steering Committee has had to ask whether the total costs envisaged are reasonable.

2   If the estimated costs are listed, we get the following:

Churches Together in England	166,000	24.60% of total
ACTS	130,000	19.25% of total
CYTUN	55,000	8.15% of total
COCBI	324,000	48.00% of total
	£675,000	

These figures have been reached by estimating what all staff costs will be if all persons are employed and paid by the new bodies, and adding the office costs, committee and activity costs and other matters detailed severally.

3   In order to estimate income we have taken as the starting point the direct cash contributions by member churches to existing councils as estimated for 1990 and adding 5% for one year's inflation.

BCC	460,000	
SCC	65,000	
CCW	38,000	(This includes an amount for the
	563,000	Covenanting Churches)
5%	28,000	
	£591,000	

It has to be noted that these are not the total budgets of the existing councils, since there are other contributions received, and some staff are seconded. **There is therefore no direct comparison between these figures and those in paragraph 2.**

4   We have had to work on the assumption that all participating churches will become members of the new bodies. This means that additional contributions from new members are to be expected. Without any firm indications at this stage, but with some preliminary conversation in Scotland, the figure we would write in is in total £120,000.

5   In total, therefore, the contributions in cash for the year 1991 may be estimated at £711,000, which should be adequate to meet the outgoings listed in paragraph 2.

6   These very preliminary estimates will need more detailed work, especially as the Commissioning Committees begin their work, and therefore should be taken at this point only as an approximation. Should any of the larger participating churches decide not to become members of the new bodies, considerable amendment to the proposals would be required.